1001 WAYS TO relax

Susannah Marriott

DK

LONDON, NEW YORK, MUNICH,
MELBOURNE, DELHI

For all my yoga teachers, past and present, with thanks

Project editor Claire Cross
Design Carole Ash at Project 360
Senior editor Helen Murray
Senior art editor Glenda Fisher
Photographer Ruth Jenkinson
Creative technical support Sonia Charbonnier
Production editor Ben Marcus
Production controller Hema Gohil
Managing editor Penny Warren
Managing art editor Marianne Markham
Jacket designer Carole Ash
Jacket editor Adam Powley
Category publisher Peggy Vance
Yoga tips Amanda Brown
Homeopathic/herbal tips Julia Linfoot BSc MCPH RSHom

Caution: if you are pregnant or have a medical condition, do not use herbs (including herbal teas) without consulting a qualified herbal practitioner. Use only the essential oils specified and never use more drops than recommended. Omit those oils suggested if pregnant or breastfeeding, or if you have high blood pressure, kidney problems or epilepsy. Some citrus oils cause photosensitivity after use when skin is exposed to sunlight. See cautions on individual recipes, and omit citrus oils if you plan to be outdoors or use a sunlamp in the six hours following use. Avoid body masks, scrubs, very hot and salt baths during pregnancy.

First published in Great Britain in 2008
by Dorling Kindersley Limited
80 Strand, London WC2R ORL
Penguin Group (UK)

A CIP catalogue record is available from the British Library.

ISBN: 978-1-4053-2802-9

Reproduced by GRB, Italy
Printed and bound by Sheck Wah Tong, China

Discover more at
www.dk.com

Contents

Introduction

When I started to write this book, I asked everyone I know how they relaxed. What a diverse range of answers I got: playing air guitar along with the Clash, growing pumpkins, brewing wine from birch trees, singing, lindy-hopping, swimming to work and making jellies. What struck me was that some weren't quiet activities, many involved nature and other people and that hardly anyone advised lounging on the sofa (or illegal substances). Contrary to received opinion, relaxing isn't about doing nothing. It's about losing yourself in an activity that works the body and takes your mind away from worries and into the present. This is a description of meditation, and you can find it on a surfboard, mountain climbing, making a hat or playing in a band.

Why do we need to relax?

Many of us lead such busy lives that we rarely switch off from the demands that trigger the stress response. When we face a threatening situation, "stress" hormones, such as adrenalin and cortisol, are released to prepare body and brain to take action: to freeze, fight or run away. The heart beats more rapidly, causing blood pressure to soar, glucose courses into the bloodstream, senses are heightened and breathing speeds up, the large muscles tense and normal functions such as digestion shut down. This is completely healthy, and may even boost immunity, if we can run away or punch out: these acts stimulate hormones that return the body to equilibrium – the relaxation response.

But how do you fight a deadline or run away from a traffic jam or tantrumming toddler? When we can't turn off stress-activated physiological responses and they stay switched on for weeks, months or years, the cardiovascular and immune systems and the brain suffer. Even more so if we fail to eat healthily, sleep or exercise enough, and resort to unhealthy coping strategies, such as smoking. Prolonged stress is linked to cardiovascular disease, metabolic syndrome (a range of symptoms including high blood pressure that are a precursor to type-2 diabetes), depression and chronic conditions such as insomnia.

What are the best ways to relax?

Easy! There are 1001 ways coming up, but in brief, approach each day with a positive mindset, eat a Mediterranean diet loaded with vegetables, fruit and oily fish, exercise most days, laugh each day, spend time in a green landscape, nurture relationships and be part of your local community. You could even get religion or volunteer. All of these bolster your defences against the negative effects of stress, helping you to be happy and relaxed – and so, amazingly, live longer. Most of all, you need an activity that transports you away from worries for more than a moment; instant gratification of the shoe-shopping variety doesn't correlate with long-term stress-relief as it leaves you feeling empty. If that meaningful pastime creates a bit of adrenalin – the tug of a fish on the hook, the shock of plunging into a cold ocean, the surge of a drum-roll – all the better as it shows your body how life should be: mostly relaxed, with an occasional shot of action to keep us on our toes!

Good luck finding whatever it is that helps you to relax.

Susannah Marriott

Susannah Marriott   Cornwall 2008

1 Destress at work

A commonly cited cause of everyday stress is work. Workers who feel under strain tend to report aching muscles, a poor appetite (or overeating), loss of sleep, physical and mental exhaustion and irritability. They also face an increased risk of heart attack, high blood pressure and cholesterol, and mental health problems. Stress should not be confused with a challenge. We benefit from challenging targets that keep the brain sharp, and when a job is well done we can bask in a relaxed state of satisfaction; this is healthy, rewarding stress. Here is a wealth of tips to convert stress into a challenge and make the working day relaxing and productive, from brain-enhancing foods and time-management ideas to ways to release tension in the body.

Starting the day

Taking time to eat a healthy, nutritious breakfast before heading off in the morning sets you up to combat any physical or mental stressors you might meet on your journey into work. Top up your anti-stress armoury for the day ahead with positive thinking and, if possible, a short period of meditation or yoga.

Make time for family and loved ones.

1

Think positive

If you approach the day feeling positive, you are less likely to suffer from symptoms of stress and to succumb to viruses circulating in the air-conditioning (stress depletes the immune system). In a 2006 study, positive thinkers were less likely to suffer colds and flu, and the colds they did get had milder symptoms. On waking, think about an event in the past that made you feel intensely happy and full of hope for the future. Bathe in those positive emotions for 2–3 minutes, letting them swell out from your heart to coat you in a protective shield from your head to your toes.

2

Rearrange your day

If you don't arrive home in the evenings until late, try to rearrange the start of your day to incorporate some relaxed family time: get up 30 minutes earlier than usual to have breakfast with the children and read them a story in the morning if you regularly miss bedtime. People who feel supported by strong family ties tend to feel more relaxed and are less likely to succumb to stress.

3

Make your own muesli

Start every day with this calming, brain-pleasing and heart-protecting combination of oats, nuts and seeds.

500g jumbo organic oats
as many nuts and seeds as you like: include Brazil nuts, chopped walnuts, pumpkin and sunflower seeds, pine nuts, sesame seeds and linseeds (flax seeds)

Pour the oats into a large jar with an air-tight lid, then add as many of the nuts and seeds as suit your palate, stirring them in until well combined. Replace the lid and store in a cool, dark place. Each morning, spoon 3–4 tbsp into a bowl and pour over semi-skimmed organic milk and 1 tbsp natural organic yogurt. Add a handful of blueberries or grapes, slices of apple or chunks of cantaloupe melon.

Keep heart and mind healthy with a fruit- and nut-laden breakfast.

4
Take a meditation class

Meditation is proven to lessen anxiety, rebalance emotions, release tension, boost immunity and fight depression. It also seems to control blood pressure at levels comparable to some medication, and boosts mental performance and memory skills. Look for an early morning class to set you up for the day.

5
Morning meditation

Sit on a rug with your legs crossed. If this is painful, sit on a yoga block or phone directory with cushions supporting your knees. Relax your hands on your thighs and close your eyes. See any thoughts as projections on a screen. Watch in a disinterested way, then imagine the screen going blank. Build up to a 20-minute session.

Prepare yourself for a stressful day with a period of silent meditation to reduce anxiety and promote calmness.

Safeguard blood vessels with a zingy lemon tonic.

6

Calming breakfast

Sugary breakfast cereals and bars cause blood-sugar levels to peak, then trough, stimulating the release of stress hormones – and feelings of anxiety, moodiness or sleepiness. Opt instead for eggs, wholegrain toast with cottage cheese or peanut butter, a fruit smoothie, porridge or some nut-laden muesli. If you do resort to grabbing something on your way to work, make it a natural yogurt and some fruit.

7

Brain-stimulant breakfast

To boost levels of the brain-activating chemical tyramine, try a bacon, ham, cheese or avocado sandwich on wholemeal bread in the morning. When you are alert and can think on your feet, you are more able to bat away sources of stress.

8

Citron pressé

Squeeze the juice of half a lemon into a glass and top up with water for a thirst-quenching, start-the-day digestive tonic that refreshes mind and body and protects your blood vessels. In addition, lemons are a rich source of vitamin C, providing extra protection against viruses circulating around the office.

9

Relaxing shower gel

When you face a particularly challenging or stressful day, wash with this blend of essential oils, which can help to focus the mind and strengthen the nerves. (Avoid during pregnancy.)

1 tbsp unscented shower gel
1 drop essential oil of juniper
2 drops essential oil of bergamot
 (FCF grade)

Place the shower gel in a small bowl and then stir in the essential oils until well combined. Use in a morning shower.

10

Sing in the shower

Singing fosters a sense of wellbeing by deepening breathing, boosting circulation and improving posture. It also prompts the release of pain-relieving endorphins that help to cancel out symptoms of stress. Let rip in the shower each morning. As you start to sing, stand taller by letting your tailbone drop and imagining the crown of your head being pulled towards the ceiling. When you inhale, visualize the breath broadening the sides of your rib cage, as if you were a fish opening your gills.

11

Start-the-day-right stretch

Stand tall, bottom tucked in, shoulders relaxing away from the ears, with your feet hip-width apart. Stretch both your arms above your head, then inhale and reach up to the sky with your right hand, stretching from your armpits up to the fingertips. Exhale and release your right arm a little, then practise the same stretch with your left hand. Repeat this stretch 10 times, alternating sides.

12

Salute the sun

Align yourself in the morning with our most potent source of power, the sun, by practising yoga's Sun Salutation sequence (see No. 541). This flowing, energetic sequence helps to build up your physical and mental stamina, which helps you maintain equilibrium throughout the day. Aim to work up to 12 repetitions at a time.

Happy commuting

A 2004 study into commuters' stress levels found that heart rate and blood-pressure levels approached those of fighter pilots, causing frustration, anxiety and even short-term amnesia. Avoid the gridlock wind-up with these antidotes to ensure that you arrive at work refreshed and alert.

13

Take control

Be productive during enforced stationary times, writing letters, processing emails or catching up on reports. Feeling in control of your time is key to remaining relaxed.

14

Window meditation

On the other hand, an enforced switch-off can be the perfect destressing tool for busy workaholics who try to shoehorn too much into a working day.

Instead of cramming on the train, leave work on your desk and use this time to stare out of the window and contemplate the world around you. Let the ever-moving flow of life in all its diversity remind you of the inconstant and changing nature of the world. Try not to focus on ideas or preoccupations. When you find yourself following thought-trails, gently switch away into this more broadened awareness.

15

Wear shades

If you have to get up in the early hours of the morning and leave for work before the sun rises to sit on a brightly lit train or bus, put on your sun shades to shield both your eyes and your brain from the harsh artificial lights. Sit back, switch off and relax until the sun comes up, then take your shades off.

Use your commute to switch off and sink into quiet contemplation.

16

Daydream solutions

If you're sick of this stressful way of life, take 10 minutes during your commute on consecutive days to contemplate other possible life options. On the first morning, let your fancy take over. Ponder all sorts of possibilities, no matter how dumb or outlandish they might seem. Could you change your job perhaps, work closer to home, move to a more manageable city, start working from home or marry a millionaire? The following day, spend another 10 minutes considering the practical ways in which you could bring about some of those solutions.

17

Lose yourself in a book

Take full advantage of precious uninterrupted reading time. These books are so engrossing that you might find yourself spending the entire day eagerly anticipating your return journey:

- *A Patchwork Planet*, Ann Tyler: begins at a railway station.
- *Trawler*, Redmond O'Hanlon: leaves you thankful that you don't commute at sea.
- *Mutant Message Down Under*, Marlo Morgan: follows a four-month trek through the terrain of the Australian outback.
- *Runaway*, Alice Munro: short

Escape journey stress: lose yourself in a sea of sound.

stories that linger in the mind, urging you to reassess your life and your relationships.

- *The Summer Book*, Tove Jansson: wise novella of life on a remote Finnish island.
- *Our Mutual Friend*, Charles Dickens: reveals the under-life of a working city.

18

Do Sudoku

Brain-teasing puzzles, such as Sudoku, give your brain a mental workout on the way into the office. Studies suggest that the logic and focus involved in such mental aerobics help to increase mental agility and even improve IQ, preparing you to tackle stressful tasks at work.

19

Music for the MP3 player

Cocoon yourself in a sea of sound. Research proves that music calms the mind and wards off anxiety and depression. Try an Indian *raga*, or melody, which takes the listener on a meditative journey. Starting slowly with an unornamented introduction to entice you and fix musical themes to the emotions, it is then paced to engage these sentiments, or *rasas*, as decorative detail, speed and volume build. As the music increases in intensity to an exhausting climax, the emotions do too until the melody hits an emotional tension-release point. Then the piece calms to a soft landing, the theme becoming imperceptible as you return to the "real" world. Look for *ragas* written for daybreak (*Bhairav, Bibhas, Jogiya, Ramkali*) or for 6–9am (*Bhupal todi, Bilaskhani todi*).

20

Walk to work

Researchers have found that a large part of the stress of commuting stems from a feeling of complete helplessness and frustration – of being pinned in by timetables, red lights and other people's bodies. The best way to combat this lack of control is to rely on your own two feet. Use the additional time it takes to walk into work to adjust your attitude, tuning into work issues and problems on the journey in and tuning out and mentally relaxing on the return leg of the journey.

21

Commute by bike

The physical benefits of cycling 2–4 hours per week have been shown to reduce stress and depression and, in studies, people who commute to work by bicycle feel more relaxed, happier and productive when they arrive at work than those who don't cycle. Enjoy some fresh air where you always have a seat!

22

Enlist a cycle mate

If you're stressed by the thought of cycling on busy city roads or fast country lanes, accompany a friend or colleague for a few mornings. Learn nifty shortcuts and places to avoid, and let your buddy motivate you. Most people find it least stressful to begin cycling in summer.

23

Join a car club

If you share a car rather than owning outright, you cut the hassle of repairs, taxing and insuring, and save money – good stress-reduction strategies. Look out for local council-supported car-share clubs or organize informally with neighbours and friends. Find out

Take control of your journey time: walk to work and avoid the rush-hour crush.

more by contacting www.zipcar.co.uk, www.streetcar.co.uk or www.citycarclub.co.uk.

24
Shout it out

When bad temper or exhaustion strike at the wheel, shout it out. Put on a rousing CD and join in – play with the melody, add harmonies and make up words. Singing allows you to soar outside your body, stuck in time and place, and to express your creativity, which is stifled in the car and maybe at work, too.

25
Zoned-out music

Relaxing driving music for lives that have to be spent in cars should include some zoned-out electronic music – try CDs by Kraftwerk, Tangerine Dream or The Necks.

26
Bumblebee breathing

This exercise is especially effective if you're fuming in traffic. Inhale normally. As you make a long exhalation, hum. Concentrate on the sound vibrating in your head. Repeat as necessary. Under the guidance of a yoga teacher, this can help to manage high blood pressure.

27
Flexible working

If commuting is a continual ordeal, contemplate working flexible hours to avoid the peak rush, or work from home one day a week. Watch your productivity rise as stress levels dip and you recoup lost working hours (the average commuter's journey time is 45–60 minutes each way).

28
Gridlock massage

If endless traffic jams make you tense and you find your shoulders scrunching around your ears when you're driving, let these quick neck and shoulder releases undo some of the negative effects of this stress.

1 With hands on your lap, inhale, pull your shoulders up, hold your breath and squeeze the muscles. Exhale forcefully and let the shoulders drop.

2 Grasp your arm with the opposite hand. Squeeze and release the flesh, working up to the shoulder and side of the neck. Repeat on the other side.

3 Place your fingertips at the bottom of the neck. Apply pressure, circling either side of the spine. Work up the neck and around to behind the ears.

Relaxing at a desk

Many of us spend longer at work than previous generations. This makes us less productive and less happy: a 2007 study found that stress hampers the brain's ability to learn and communicate, causing memory problems and depression. To guard against this, neuroscientists urge us to eat brain-enhancing foods, make time for exercise and relaxation and use destressing techniques at work. Preserve your health and sanity with these strategies.

29

Pimp your cubicle

Separated work stations bring anonymity and a tendency to put your head down and ignore fellow workers. "Sterile", or personality-free, offices were blamed in a Timotei study for stress in office workers. Step outside your cubicle to make human contact, and try to personalize your space with photos, mementos and plants.

30

Pin up a poem

A good poem compresses complex thoughts into a few lines, and so makes a good escape from work and a reviving workout for both the brain and the emotions. You can't do better than Shakespeare's sonnets – try numbers 12 (about time) and 27 (about journeying in your head). Stick one to the computer monitor or lavatory door and contemplate how few words are necessary for impact and how meaning can shift from one word to the next.

Personalize your work space with calming reminders of life away from work.

31

Have a laugh

Numerous studies have reported that laughing can help to counter stress and relieve pain as well as giving the immune system a welcome boost. And the benefits of laughter are communal. Your own laughter triggers activity in the brains of those who hear it, causing them to laugh in response, found a 2006 study in the *Journal of Neuroscience*. Be the one who defuses conflict and builds morale by telling a corny joke.

32
Raise a spider plant
If environmental hazards in offices worry you, grow a spider plant. They thrive on pollutants: one study found that they cut indoor pollution by up to 87 per cent in 24 hours.

33
Munch on apricots
Eat a handful of dried apricots every day. These are a good source of potassium, which helps to control blood pressure.

34
Avocado snack
Packed with vitamin B_6, avocado can help to keep you calm when stress hormones are sending co-workers

Zap office pollutants with a cleansing spider plant.

crazy. Slice in half, de-stone, add a dash of balsamic vinegar, a little salt and pepper, and eat with a teaspoon.

35
Enjoy a bowl of berries
Top superfood, blueberry, is rich in antioxidants: reservatrol helps to repair damage done by free radicals (unstable molecules produced as a result of stress) and pterostilbene regulates blood-sugar levels, inhibiting the release of stress hormones. And they keep better than other berries.

36
Have a cup of tea
In a 2006 study, men who drank black tea's blend of antioxidant ingredients recovered more quickly from the effects of stress than those

Packed with antioxidants, blueberries balance blood sugar, keeping stress at bay.

who did not, and felt more relaxed up to 50 minutes later. A study at King's College, London, showed that drinking around three cups a day enhances mental performance.

37
Enjoy coffee
As well as boosting mental acuity, a 2006 report found that 1–2 cups a day of coffee relieves liver stress, supporting the liver's detox functions and helping stabilize blood sugar. It may also relax muscles, ease pain and cut the risk of heart disease and stroke.

38
Plan a workout
Exercise offsets stress by stimulating neuron growth in the part of the brain linked with memory loss. Plan 30–60 minutes' exercise most days.

39
Flower remedies for work

The following can ease a bad day. Place 4 drops in water and sip until symptoms subside. In extreme cases, place directly on your tongue:

• Hornbeam eases 'Monday morning' feeling, when you're feeling stale or lacking enthusiasm.

• Impatiens reduces headless-chicken syndrome: when there is so much on that you miss the bigger picture.

• Walnut offers protection from unpleasant atmospheres or people and is invaluable for sensitive types.

40
Destress your spine

Stand with your right sole on a chair. Put your left hand on your right knee, twist your right shoulder back and let the spine follow. Exhale, and turn a bit more. Inhale back to the centre and repeat on the other side.

41
Relax your upper body

You don't have to leave your chair to experience a reviving stretch. Do this sequence after the leg stretches, below, to relax the whole body.

Sit back with the top of your seat digging in below your shoulder blades. Take your hands behind the chair and arch backwards, sliding your hands down the legs or sides of the chair. Don't drop your head right back as this can strain the neck. Come up carefully.

Slide your bottom forwards, widen your knees and plant your feet on the floor. Fold your arms onto the table and lean forwards, extending out of the hips. To lengthen the spine, you may have to move the chair back. Come up carefully.

42
Stretch your legs

When you're feeling frazzled, stand up for a few minutes to stretch out tense muscles. Before you start, concentrate on your breathing for a moment, letting it become smooth and steady.

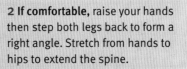

1 Put your hands on the desk, bend the right knee and step the left leg back. Press the left heel down to stretch the calf. Repeat on the other side.

2 If comfortable, raise your hands then step both legs back to form a right angle. Stretch from hands to hips to extend the spine.

3 Put your foot on the table, or chair if this is too high, legs straight, toes flexing in. If comfortable, stretch up your arms. Repeat on the other leg.

Stress-reduction kit

When you're too busy to stop, carry around some calming essentials. Healthy snacks and drinks are an especially good way to support the body and mind through stressful periods. According to the British Heart Foundation, if you have an existing health condition, such as high blood pressure or diabetes, it's even more important to take such self-help measures to lessen the effects of workplace stress.

Carry a favourite moisturizing cream to nourish your skin.

43
Calm and clear head
Australian Bush Flower essence Calm and Clear is excellent if you over commit, bringing the mental clarity so elusive to the chronically busy.

44
Photos that make you sigh
Looking at photos of loved ones boosts endorphins and positivity.

45
Red grapes
Keep a stash to repair damage caused by free radicals. The skins contain the antioxidant reservatrol, which accounts for the benefits of red wine.

46
A bottle of water
Staying hydrated helps you to keep a clear head. Students who drink water in tests achieve better results.

47
White tea bags
White tea has even more polyphenol antioxidants than green tea, helping to ward off heart disease and stroke and boost immunity to protect against opportunist bugs. Carry individually wrapped sachets.

48
Emergency banana
Bananas contain B vitamins, essential for the nervous system as well as the healthy functioning of brain cells and energy production.

49
Good dark chocolate
A little dark chocolate is a pick-me-up with a potent antioxidant punch. Its antioxidant flavonoids relax blood vessels, which boosts blood flow and reduces high blood pressure. Opt for varieties with 70 per cent cocoa solids, which taste best and sate the appetite.

50
Herbal tea bags
- Camomile tea has a similar effect on the brain to anti-anxiety drugs.
- Peppermint tea helps to calm digestive problems and headaches.
- Ginger tea quells nausea related to late nights and overwork.
- Fennel tea rebalances the digestion and stimulates an appetite.

51
Calming skin food
Carry a soothing skin cream to counter the effects of chilly winds. In hot offices, use this as a balm for dry lips and cuticles.

52
Nail buffer
A two-minute buffing brings fresh blood and nutrients to nails. Caring for nails stops you nibbling them!

53
Scent refreshment
Place 1 drop of essential oil of peppermint on a tissue and put in a plastic bag. Take a sniff if you feel down, mentally fatigued or angry. (Avoid if pregnant or breastfeeding.)

54
Fabulous notebook
Carry a notebook to jot inspiring thoughts before they fry in a frazzled brain. Find one made from handmade paper with a leather or cloth binding.

55
Old-fashioned ink pen
Simply having something well made and old fashioned makes you feel like you live a leisurely existence. Invest in a lovely pen and savour writing longhand rather than typing.

56
Writing exercises
Escape daily frustrations by writing in your notebook for 10 minutes. Don't think too hard or get hung up on grammar: this allows your creative side to let rip. Try the following:
- my bedroom when I was eight
- my grandparents' house
- I love spring because…
- my favourite room
- my first memory
- my worst holiday

Equip yourself with essential stress busters to get you through hectic days.

Relaxation windows

When you feel overwhelmed, stopping everything for a few minutes preserves your peace of mind. At stressful times, down tools and take time out to eat or drink something sustaining, or to take some brisk exercise or a power nap. When you return, see how much more focused you feel and how much more measured your reactions are to everyday stressors. Taking time to relax makes you more resourceful and protects you from the negative effects of stress.

Break from your desk: have lunch out.

57

Stop every hour

If you are working on a relentless task, set an alarm clock to bleep on the hour. Break off and check if you are still working productively. Note if you have drifted into daydream mode. Take a few seconds to refocus your priorities.

58

Eat an oat cake

All complex carbohydrates have a calming effect, but oats have more profoundly relaxing properties, and

are recommended by herbalists to treat nervous exhaustion, anxiety and insomnia. If you feel "nervy", reach for an oat cake or two.

59

Snack on nuts and seeds

Nuts and seeds have a sedative effect on the brain. Keep a mix in your drawer to nibble in a break, including in it almonds, hazelnuts and sunflower and sesame seeds. These are high in proteins that contain the amino acid tryptophan, which helps to make serotonin, the chemical that creates a feeling of contented calmness.

60

Take a lunch break

In an American study, just 3 per cent of people took a full hour for lunch. Britons spend an average 27 minutes away from their desk, with women

less likely to take a break, and a Reuters' report suggests that Europe is fast catching up. A long-hours' culture that glues you to a desk can frazzle your brain and hamper performance, so take a break.

61

Get away from your desk

Another American study found that 75 per cent of those who take a lunchbreak sit at their desks to eat, and many don't eat at all. For this reason, some Canadian government workers are obliged to take an hour's break away from work. See the difference it makes when you dine in a café or picnic in the park.

62

Relaxing lunches

Opt for a light meal that is nerve-calming, brain-supportive and energizing, such as the following:

- celery, carrot and cucumber crudités with hummus
- salads made up of lettuce, spinach leaves, avocados and walnuts
- seaweed-wrapped sushi
- baked potatoes
- oily fish, such as sardines, with wholemeal bread
- chicken sandwich, salad or soup

63
Add olive oil

Drizzle some olive oil over the leaves of your lunchtime salad. As well as relaxing blood vessels, which helps to boost the circulation, olive oil seems to protect the brain from declining performance, helping to combat the post-lunch "slump".

64
Stress-fighting nutrients

When you are up against it, your body requires more nutrients, since many essential vitamins and minerals are depleted by stress. When work is particularly demanding, fill up on extra fruit and vegetables, which are a good source of potassium and vitamin C, and on seafood and wholegrains, which contain zinc – the first three nutrients to be lost.

Avoid the "pm slump" with light, re-energizing meals such as fresh sushi.

65
Enjoy curry

Spices help to regulate insulin, in turn quelling anxiety. Try dishes with turmeric, cloves and cinnamon.

66
Afternoon pick-me-up

A fresh fruit salad is stress-reducing when it contains cantaloupe or honeydew melon, apricots, bananas or watermelon, which contain blood pressure-regulating potassium. Top with creamy natural yogurt and a topping of toasted seeds.

67
Stock up on B12

Lack of vitamin B_{12}, which occurs naturally in foods of animal origin, hampers the nervous system, leading to stress-related problems. If you don't eat meat, fish, eggs or dairy regularly, eat more at stressful times, or eat yeast spread on bread.

68

Sky gazing

On a clear day, leave the building for 15 minutes and find a patch of grass. Lie on your back and close your eyes. Then look at the sky. Think about how vast and endless it is, and imagine that your mind is similarly infinite. Watch a cloud move across the sky and out of sight. Think of thoughts and feelings as clouds that pass through your mind but move on. They are not your mind and so cannot have a long-term impact on it. After 10 minutes, close your eyes for a moment, then roll onto your right side and slowly stand up.

69

Drink spa water

Water drawn from sources rich in minerals is reputed to have calming, curative properties. Look for varieties that come from traditional sources of thermal healing.

70

Shut your mouth

Vow not to talk for a brief period each day, maybe while you eat or as you process emails. While you are silent, turn off outside distractions, such as the radio. As you learn to stay silent on the outside, notice how crazy and active your inner voice remains, and work on trying to make that less mouthy, too.

71

Grab some exercise

Activating the body by strolling briskly around the block eases muscle tension and releases anxiety. Just 10 minutes of exercise has been shown to bring back *joie de vivre*, lift anxiety and dissipate lethargy. One study showed that this could even spark a two-hour burst of productivity in the afternoon. While striding out, plan how you can fit a 45-minute session of more intense aerobic activity into your day to elevate your mood, reduce blood pressure, increase energy levels and relieve symptoms of stress on a long-term basis.

72

Breathe easy

When tense and stressed, many people unknowingly hold their breath. Take a break of a few minutes and try this exercise to rebalance your breathing. Close your eyes and notice the air flowing in through your nostrils. As the air enters your lungs, watch your diaphragm drop and your rib cage widen. Keep watching as your chest contracts and the air flows out through your nostrils. Repeat the process, maintaining a constant focus on your breathing. Let it exclude everything else from your thoughts. This is inner peace, and it's this easy to find.

Keep a glass of water to hand to stay hydrated and replenish lost minerals.

73

Find a place of retreat

If you have a prayer room at your place of work or study, think about getting into the habit of praying, or otherwise simply spend some time sitting and quietly reflecting, at regular times throughout the day. If it helps, try to think of this not as a time of spiritual devotion but as a recharging break, taking you away from the stresses of the workplace for a few moments, which in turn helps to rebalance your mind and renew your energy. The traditional Muslim times of prayer – dawn, noon, mid-afternoon, sunset and nightfall – make good times to sit quietly, turn within and broaden your focus away from yourself. You could start by giving thanks, extending love to those you care for or contemplating themes such as forgiveness or peace.

74
Tea leaf divination
This makes a diverting break with colleagues you know well, especially if you are feeling uncertain about the future.

3–4 tsp loose-leaf black tea
medium-sized teapot
teacups and saucers
milk or slices of lemon and sugar,
  to taste

Spoon the tea into a warmed pot, then fill the pot to the top with just-boiled water. Leave the tea to steep for five minutes, then pour it into the cups (do not use a strainer), adding a little milk or lemon and sugar if you wish.
Place each teacup on a saucer. Put your feet up and enjoy the tea and a chat. When you have drunk the tea, upturn the cup on the saucer and turn it clockwise three times.
Turn the cup back the right way up and hand it to a colleague to analyse. She might look for arrows that suggest a future direction in your life, footprints or hearts, ships or suitcases, figures or dollar signs. See if you can find interpretations to fit the various images.

75
Start a sketchbook
Buy an artist's sketchbook and selection of pencils of varying hardness (ask in an art materials shop for advice). When you feel in need of a break, pick up your sketch pad and draw whatever you see. You might discover that you like to specialize in portraits of people or animals, in recording the changing seasons through one window or in sketching still-life collections of objects. Don't obsess about being a skilled artist: simply appreciate the alternative viewpoint this activity gives you on the world.

76
Build in rewards
If life is all demands and few rewards, spoil yourself with a treat "window" every day: walk to the florist to choose a bunch of flowers, make a detour to pass the best patisserie in town, call a friend for a quick catch-up or snatch a chapter of an engrossing novel.

77
Become a mentor
Studies suggest that giving skills back to your community really does help to make you feel happier and more relaxed (people who volunteer live longer, too). Find out whether your employer runs a mentor scheme, or get in contact with your local youth services and see if you can help a teenager towards a career in your industry.

Broaden your awareness: build in regular moments throughout the day for quiet reflection to recharge flagging energy levels.

Relaxing tense hands

Restless hands and ragged nails are tell-tale signs of a hassled mind, and repetitive strain injury a hazard for those who have to repeat the same task continually during the working day. Easing out stiff hands is an easy route to releasing strain in other parts of the body, since nerve endings in the palms relate to key spots where we store tension, such as the neck and shoulders.

Treat yourself to a lunchtime pampering session and feel tension ebb away.

78
Cosset with cashmere

If your hands get tense because they are cold, the tendons and ligaments become more prone to injury. Try wearing thin fingerless gloves while you are typing – look for ones in pure new wool, cashmere or silk (which fits the hand like a second skin), which are nature's most heat-retentive materials.

Add a healthy glow to nails with oil of evening primrose.

79
Get a manicure

A hand primping session releases tension in the face and shoulders, too. Choose salons with "holistic" products, free from formaldehyde and toluene, a chemical linked with fatigue, weakness and confusion.

80
Lunchtime nail bath

Add 1 tsp olive oil and lemon juice to warm water. The oil replenishes moisture lost due to central heating, while the lemon eliminates stains and has a rejuvenating aroma. Relax with your fingertips immersed for 10–15 minutes.

81
Rejuvenating nail oil

To strengthen weak nails and bring a rosy glow and sheen that shouts "I am not stressed", use these oils for a nourishing lunchtime massage.

1 tbsp grapeseed oil
1 capsule evening primrose oil
1 tsp avocado or wheatgerm oil
2 drops essential oil of neroli
   or sandalwood

Mix the oils, then massage into the nails. Slip on cotton gloves if you need to type afterwards.

82
Qi-gung breathing

In this exercise you connect with the grounding element earth and the element of inspiration, air. This can help you feel more able to tackle potential sources of tension.
Stand tall, the soles of your feet rooting into the earth and the top of your head extending to the heavens. Extend your arms to the sides. Turn your right palm to face upwards.
Breathe in; imagine inhaling

through your right palm, sucking in energy. Feel it travel across into your left palm. As you exhale, let the energy drain into the floor, centring and earthing you. Continue for three minutes if comfortable.

83
Eat crunchy coleslaw

A 2006 study found a diet high in vitamin K (found in leafy greens) decreases the risk of joint damage in the hands. Take in this vitamins K- and B-rich coleslaw for lunch. Makes enough for two.

½ cabbage, shredded
2 tbsp Swiss chard or spinach, shredded
1 large organic carrot, grated
1 tart apple, peeled and grated
handful raisins, optional
3–4 tbsp mayonnaise
freshly ground black pepper, to taste

In a bowl mix the cabbage, spinach or chard with the carrot, apple and raisins. Add mayonnaise and pepper.

84
Computer set-up

Position your keyboard so that your elbows are at right angles to your upper arms, and the wrists are level (not sloping up, down or to the side). Resist resting your wrists on the desk; it may help to prop up the keyboard. When you stop typing rest your hands, and take frequent rests to circle your shoulders and wrists and shake out tension in your fingers.

85
Ditch the mouse

To keep your hands destressed, use keyboard commands instead of mouse pointing. Learning the commands exercises the brain, too.

86
Origami cup

Make a paper cup that holds water! This exercises your brain and rests the fingers, helping to maintain dexterity if you spend hours at the same activity, which can lead to occupational overuse injuries.

1 Fold a square of paper into a triangle with the two "free" points at the top. Fold the points across to meet their opposite edge.

2 Fold the top point of the triangle down and crease the fold. Turn the paper over and repeat this fold on the other side.

3 Press together the sides to open the cup. Stand the cup on a surface, fill half way with some cool water and enjoy a refreshing drink.

Flex your wrists and centre your energy with this grounding prayer position.

hands clockwise, then anti-clockwise, then in both directions. Finish by shaking out the hands.

91
Wrist and finger stretch

Extend your arms, pointing the hands down at the wrists. Take five breaths in and out then point the fingers up for five breaths. Interlink the fingers, turn the palms out and straighten the arms.

92
Destressing hand release

Sit and rest your palms downwards on your thighs, fingers slightly spread. Close your eyes. Make the elbows heavy and feel the wrists drop and shoulders release. Let the hands sink as if resting in sand, with their contours supported. With each exhalation feel the hands spreading.

87
Take a break

Stretching the hand muscles helps to prevent injuries, which are more likely when hands are static. Use the exercises here at least once an hour when carrying out repetitive tasks, such as typing, lifting heavy pans or playing an instrument.

88
Prayer position

With palms together and thumbs at the breastbone, press each finger into its partner. Inhale and feel the warmth in the chest. Exhale, and take the palms as low as you can before they separate. Hold for five full breaths in and out.

89
Self-help acupressure

The thumb joint often holds tension as it is one of the few places in the hand where there is muscle and a tendon. Support one hand with the other, palms facing upwards. Use the bottom thumb to massage the base of the top thumb, easing into areas of soreness. Swap hands and repeat.

90
Wrist mobilizer

Let the hands droop from the wrists and shake them up and down and from side to side to loosen the joint. With your hands at chest height and the elbows soft, slowly draw circles, moving from the wrist. Circle both

93
Hand chakra exercise

Stimulating an energy centre in the palm is thought by yogis to make communication more relaxed.
Rub your palms then hold them apart, facing each other.
Slowly move your palms closer until you feel resistance or warmth. Move them back and forth to sense the energy: imagine it as a tennis-ball shaped sphere of light. Then sit with eyes closed and palms facing upwards and sense the energy for 30 seconds.

Releasing stiff feet

Long hours standing leads to tired, sore feet, creating tension that shows as strain on the face and causes postural and back problems. Simply standing correctly can be the key to releasing tension. Once your feet no longer grip the floor and your bodyweight is distributed equally, aches and pains in the lower back, shoulders and neck melt away.

Enjoy the sensation of going barefoot and the unfamiliar contact with the ground.

94
Solid roots

Take your shoes off and stand with your feet wide apart and your knees soft. If you can balance, close your eyes. Otherwise, fix your gaze and slightly lower your eyelids. Let your arms hang loose. Feel your feet against the floor, noticing the areas where you take more weight – you might find a difference between one foot and the other (think about how your shoes wear and spots of hard skin). Tilt your body to even the pressure. Imagine connecting with everything under you: floorboards, foundations, soil, rock, underground strata and waterways, caves, lava. Feel the ground support you. The whole world in fact. Breathe.

95
Go barefoot

Kick off your shoes whenever you can to allow your feet to breathe and expand, making contact with the floor with all four corners (both sides of the heels and the base of the big and little toes).

96
Use a foot roller

Buy a foot roller to keep at work. Massage your feet every hour, working into sore or gritty patches.

97
Warm your feet

Wool is the most insulating material. Protect cold feet with luxurious cashmere or wool socks (choose "pure new" wool). Top with sheepskin slippers or boots.

Keep a foot roller handy to smooth away tension from tired, achy feet.

98
Analgesic foot soak

If you have to stand for long periods, try this soothing footbath. The analgesic properties of mustard relieve aching bones.

1 heaped tbsp mustard powder
1 bucket
1 large knobbly pebble

Make a smooth paste with water and the powder. Fill a bucket with warm water, add the paste, then plunge in your feet and calves for 15 minutes. Drop in the pebble and use this to massage tender areas on your soles.

99

Warming footbath

If sitting for hours chills your feet, add some chopped fresh ginger root to a warming lunchtime footbath.

Destress aching feet with a warm, herb-infused footbath.

100

Soothing herbal footbath

Add 1 tsp of each of the following tinctures to a bowl of warm water, or toss in some rose petals, then soak your feet, if possible during a break or else once you return home.
- Marigold (*Calendula officinalis*) offers antifungal properties while soothing sore or cracked skin.
- Red clover (*Trifolium pratense*) helps to heal skin conditions such as eczema or psoriasis.
- Witch hazel (*Hamamelis virginiana*) used for sprains, bruises, skin blemishes and varicose veins.

101

Swollen feet remedy

Prolonged standing (and being pregnant) can lead to swelling of the feet as fluid pools in the tissues (known as oedema). Combat this by taking 2 tablets of Nat.Mur tissue salts four times daily.

102

Lunchtime pedicure

For those who spend hours standing, a pedicure brings welcome lightness to tired lower limbs by eliminating fatigue, improving circulation and reducing fluid retention. Look for treatments that offer footbaths, exfoliation and massage, rather than those that specialize in special effects for nails.

103

Book a reflexology session

Reflexologists don't just massage your feet. By analysing zones on the feet that correspond to other parts of the body, they diagnose stress-related ailments and treat them by exerting pressure on reflex points.

104

Releasing stiff ankles

Sit on a chair with bare feet. Pick up one foot, and cross the ankle over the opposite knee. Hold your ankle with one hand. With the other hand, grasp the foot and slowly circle it a few times. Repeat on the other foot.

105

Arch reviver

Stand near a support with your shoes off and feet hip-width apart. Lift high onto your tiptoes. Keeping on tiptoes and with a straight back, lower your knees and descend as low as possible. Don't let your heels drop! Lift back to upright and only then let your heels drop down. Take a rest, then rise and slowly repeat.

106

Legs-up-the-wall yoga pose

Try this pose to relax the back and legs. It requires clear wall and floor space. If you have an office, shut the door, or do it at home after work.

Curl up on your side, knees bent and bottom near to the wall. Swing your legs up the wall, keeping your trunk aligned with your legs.

Take your arms to the side with palms up and relax for five minutes. If your legs are uncomfortable or bent, move your bottom further from the wall until it feels right.

107

Stretch your toes

These stretches are unbeatable for stiff, scrunched-up feet. If you find them fairly demanding, try to breathe through the discomfort.

1 Take your shoes off and kneel on the floor, next to a wall for balance. For extra comfort, place a folded blanket under your knees.

2 Step one foot forwards and tuck the toes of your back foot under. Slowly lower your bottom towards your back heel. Breathe out.

3 Relax your back foot. Roll your front foot forwards, pressing the knuckles into the floor. If possible, roll around on the bones. Repeat the other side.

Smoothing out lines

Constant worry etches our cares onto our faces in the form of frown lines and drooping mouths. Stress increases the production of free radicals, implicated in ageing, and so the complexion suffers a double whammy if we don't relax. The stress hormone cortisol also delays skin repair by diverting blood flow and nutrients from the skin to fuel the brain and muscles to fight or flee from stress. Here are ways to switch on the antidote: the body's relaxation response.

108
Eat fat

Feelings of irritability and moodiness may be the result of low levels of omega-3 fatty acids in your diet. To restore a sense of emotional equilibrium and in turn help to relax a furrowed forehead, snack on walnuts and lunch on small oily fish, such as sardines and mackerel, at least twice a week.

Protect skin with nutrient-rich foods, such as salmon and brightly coloured vegetables.

109
Skin-repair foods

Foods rich in vitamins A, C and E and the B vitamins help to combat free-radical damage and repair skin. Find these vitamins in abundance in eggs, dairy produce, oily fish such as salmon, liver, brightly coloured fresh fruit and vegetables and dark green leafy vegetables, whole grains, nuts and legumes.

110
Crunch an apple

Apples contain high amounts of the antioxidant flavonoid quercetin, and working your jaw over a particularly crisp, tart variety challenges stress in the jaw and lips.

111
Stress-relieving facial oils

These oils are rich in antioxidants, which help to fight damage done to the skin by stress-induced free radicals. Look for them in commercial skincare products and apply a little to massage away frown lines:

- olive oil
- rosehip oil
- argun oil
- grapeseed oil
- moringa oil

112
Soothing facial oil

Try these massaging oils, renowned for their wrinkle-reducing properties. (Avoid in pregnancy.)

2 tbsp grapeseed oil
1 capsule evening primrose oil

4 drops each essential oils of
rosewood and frankincense

Pour the oils into a dark glass bottle
then drop in the essential oils. Seal
and store in a cool dark place. Shake
well before use.

113
Hot and bothered tonic

Keep a facial water spray in the
fridge. When hot and bothered, give
your face and neck a fine misting.

114
Cooling eye gel

Keep eye gel in the fridge to apply
when you feel stressed, circling the
eyes with your ring fingers.

115
Quick facial check

When you finish a task, check your
expression. Are your frowning or
squinting? Are your lips pursed and
jaw set? Reset your expression,
adopting a slight smile and long
neck. Feel how this lightens cares.

116
Brow rub

To relax a furrowed forehead, place
both index fingers in the centre of
the forehead, above the eyebrows,
fingertips facing. Rub the pads of the
fingers towards each other and back
again. Work up to the hairline.

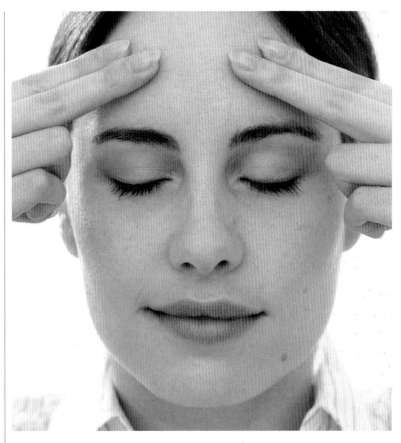

Rejuvenate tired skin with an antioxidant-rich facial oil.

117
Smoothing strokes

With the edge of your index fingers,
stroke from the eyebrow to the hair
in a stream of stress-lifting strokes.
Work to one side of the forehead,
back to centre and to the other side.

118
Lion pose

Screw up your face like a prune –
best to do this in the rest room!
Open your eyes and mouth as wide
as you can. Exhaling, stick out your
tongue and look upwards. Add a
roaring "haaah" sound for extra
benefits. Relax and enjoy a tingling
sense of rejuvenation, especially if
you tend to purse your lips.

119
Face palming

Briskly rub your palms together
until they tingle. Place them over
your eyes. Feel energy coursing into
the eyes and forehead, relaxing any
hardness. Palm your cheeks and jaw,

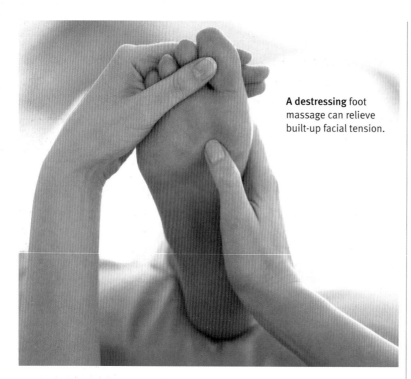

A **destressing** foot massage can relieve built-up facial tension.

123
Treat your feet
Stress on the soles shows on the face. Massaging your feet in a break (or even better being given a foot massage) can act like a mini facelift.

124
Undoing negative thoughts
Thinking the worst of events can cause downcast lines by the mouth. Recast your thoughts to soften facial tension. If you think negatively, step back and ask: are you being over-critical or making assumptions?

125
Post-it reflection
Stick this quote from medieval mystic Julian of Norwich on your monitor: "…all shall be well, and all shall be well, and all manner of things shall be well." Ponder its optimism, compassion and universal focus. Try it as a mantra: close your eyes, say the first part silently as you inhale and the second as you exhale.

bathing in the residual energy. Stimulating the hand chakra in this way is said to reconnect you to the organs of action, which can help you to avoid unnecessary effort.

120
Try Indian head massage
Massaging the head undoes tight neck and shoulder muscles that restrict circulation to the scalp and face. Let an Indian head massage therapist press and release the scalp and use percussive hand movements to ease tension and bring a relaxed glow. By applying pressure to key energy points, the therapist restores a flow of subtle energy to boost the body's natural healing powers.

121
Get a lunchtime facial
Lying in a dark room for 45 minutes while someone cleanses, massages and applies scented unguents to your face can't be beaten for melting furrowed brows. Look for lunchtime specials with two or three therapists working on feet, face and hands.

122
Deep-heat hair treatment
"Biostructure" salons rejuvenate hair stressed by heat, colour and styling products (especially if used with hairdryers). The polyfiller-like action that "rebonds" hair and puts back moisture lifts facial stress, too.

126
Spacious thinking
Approach each experience with an open mind. Picture it as a beautiful vista. Don't paste in past assumptions; see it for what it is. This helps you to stay detached from outcomes if you tend to be critical or worry in advance.

127
Autogenic training
Inveterate worriers could consider autogenic training. In sessions you are taught to replace stress reactions with a relaxation response similar to meditation. This can ease symptoms of stress, from anxiety and insomnia to muscular pain and panic attacks.

128
Worry essence
Australian Bush Flower Essence Crowea suits chronic worriers and those who feel destabilized by anxiety, restoring calm and balance. It is also used to treat stomach ulcers. Place 4 drops in a glass of water and sip until symptoms subside. In extreme cases, place the drops directly on the tongue.

See each moment like an open space: a new experience to be explored.

129
Homeopathy for worriers
Try the following remedies:
- Ars.Alb 30 for people whose main worries are about money or health.
- Calc.carb 30 for those stressed by responsibility who dwell on trivial worries to avoid thinking about important stuff. Suits people who fear losing their mental faculties.
- Staphisagria 30 for those who feel unable to assert themselves when unfairly treated, and all who hold in anger and rehearse conversations or arguments over and over.

130
Stress-release acupressure
Located on your forehead are two stress-release points, found on the bumps at either side of the upper forehead. Use the right thumb and middle finger, held 5cm (2in) apart, to find the bumps. If you're gentle you may feel the area almost before you touch it. Gently touch here to feel calmer.

131
Jaw release
Locate where the jaw hinges in front of the ears. Clench your teeth to check it is the right spot: the muscles should twitch. This is the temperomandibular joint, responsible for tension in the jaw. Use the first and second fingers to rub it in circular movements. Apply as much pressure as is comfortable.

Upper body release

We tend to store tension around the neck and shoulders as a result of bad posture. This might be caused by spending time immobile at a computer, with a phone clenched between chin and shoulder, or by the stress response that unconsciously causes us to brace the muscles in the neck and shoulders ready to punch someone or run away. When this isn't relieved it can lead to chronic pain.

The **calming properties** of lavender oil help to smooth away tension and stress in stiff muscles.

132
Assess your breath
Shallow breathing collapses the chest, hunching shoulders and back. To re-establish deep breathing, put one hand on the abdomen and one on the chest. Breathe and see which hand moves most. If it's the top one, you're not breathing deeply. Exhale deep into the abdomen and observe your lower hand moving in and out.

133
Look up
Feeling preoccupied makes us drop the head and collapse the chest. Walk looking up and forwards, your gaze about 20 feet away. Imagine gliding to that point on a moving walkway.

134
Check your chin
Are you leading movements with your head? Perhaps your chin juts forwards in an urge to be busy or to lead? This strains the neck and shoulders, and the lower back and jaw. Draw your chin in and position your ears over your shoulders for a more relaxed, natural posture.

135
Soften your jaw
Check your jaw and teeth for tension at regular times in the day. If you habitually clench, soften your mouth, making sure your lips are softly closed and your tongue rests lightly on the top of your palate.

136
Easy sitting
The least stressful position for working at a computer is with elbows at right angles to the upper arms and shoulders relaxed. Position the monitor so that you face directly forwards (try placing it further away and lower than usual), then draw in your chin slightly to lengthen the back of your neck.

137
Quick body release
Lie on your back with your knees bent and your feet flat on the floor. Cross your arms over your chest and give yourself a hug. Then gently start to rock your upper body from side to side for a minute or so. Swap to the opposite cross of your arms and repeat the action.

138
Gentle swing out
Stand with your feet hip-width apart and allow your arms to relax by your sides. With your knees slightly bent, start to sway your arms gently from side to side and gradually follow this movement with your upper body, bending your knees and turning to look over each shoulder as you sway. Don't force yourself into a twist; keep everything soft and loose.

139
Shoulder opener

Stand feet hip-width apart. Hold a long belt or scarf in both hands with the hands 1m apart. Inhaling, keep the tension on the belt and raise your arms over your head and behind the back. Don't bend your arms or twist your shoulders. If it's tight, widen the grip; if easy, bring the hands closer. Exhale and bring your arms back. Repeat a few times. (Stop if the neck tenses.)

140
Aching muscle rub

Massage these oils into aching shoulders. (Avoid if you are pregnant, have high blood pressure or epilepsy.)

3 tbsp olive oil
8 drops essential oil of lavender
4 drops essential oil of rosemary

Pour the olive oil into a bowl, add the essential oils and stir well.

141
Take Alexander lessons

One-to-one lessons with an Alexander Technique teacher re-educate you to release tension in your large muscles and let underlying musculature support the body. This allows more effortless movement, balance, co-ordination and thought processes. Book an introductory lesson with a few teachers to find one you can work with long-term.

142
Gomukhasana arms

Stand or sit and hold a belt or scarf in one hand and take it over your head. Bend the arm and drop the hand behind your head, between the shoulders. Bring the other hand up behind the back to catch hands or

Challenge your upper body with this bracing arm stretch.

the belt. Stretch one elbow to the ceiling, the other to the floor. Release and repeat on the other side.

143
Try Feldenkrais classes

The Feldenkrais Method teaches you how to move with ease and without straining yourself by raising your awareness of movement, posture and breathing. As well as bringing relief from chronic muscular tension and pain, most people find this technique improves their posture and co-ordination in everyday activities. In classes, you lie on the floor and follow a series of simple and slow directed movements that reveal your unhelpful habits, built up over years, and help you to find new, more positive ways of moving.

144
Head rolls

Stand or sit upright and drop your chin to your chest. Roll your head to the side, your ear dropping to the shoulder. Roll back and repeat to the other side. Don't roll the head back, and rely on the weight of your head (not force) to create the stretch.

145
Breath release

This calms the emotions while stretching the shoulders and chest. **Stand** feet hip-width apart. Watch your breathing. Hug your arms over your chest, fingers hooking over the shoulder blades. Drop your head. **Inhaling**, raise the head and stretch out the arms. Feel this opening your heart and arching the upper back. **Exhaling**, cross the arms again and drop your head. Repeat a few times, changing the cross of your arms.

146
Pilates shoulder release

This deceptively simple exercise isolates movement in the shoulder blades, settling them into a healthy position that relieves tension.

1 Stand with heels and head against a wall, elbows at your sides and arms bent in an L-shape, palms up. Breathe the abdominal muscles back and up.

2 Take your forearms out to the side, towards the wall. Feel a pinch between your shoulder blades. Hold, engaging the abdominal muscles.

3 Bring your forearms back to the starting position. Repeat the whole sequence for 30–60 seconds and then shake out your arms.

Easing the lower back

Research by America's National Institute for Occupational Safety and Health demonstrates that stress at work increases the risk of suffering musculoskeletal disorders of the back and upper body. Physiotherapists blame badly fitting office chairs, inactivity, obesity and tension. One of the best ways to prevent back pain is to exercise most days and pay attention to good posture basics.

147
Watch your posture
If your job involves standing, make sure your posture allows the body's major muscles to relax. Adopt a firm base, with feet hip-width apart and toes pointing forwards. Lift up, positioning your knees and hips over your ankles. Tilt your pelvis forwards slightly and scoop your abdomen in and up (without holding your breath). Then lift from hips to armpits and relax your shoulders over your hips. Draw your shoulder blades together and down and lengthen the crown of your head towards the ceiling.

148
Sitting well
When sitting to work, make sure both feet are flat to the floor and the backs of your thighs are well supported by the seat. Imagine your tailbone dropping, the head rising and space between each vertebra.

149
Please adjust your chair
Badly adjusted office chairs are an all too common cause of lower back problems. Use an office chair that you can adjust to suit your particular frame. Position the height of the chair so that your feet are flat on the floor, and move the back of the seat to a position that offers good support to your lower back. Then sit so that your shoulders balance over your hips, and your ears align with your shoulders.

150
Hone your core
Before bending, lifting or turning, focus on your abdomen. Scoop your tailbone slightly and exhale your stomach muscles towards your lower back. This engages the "core" muscles that support your structure and safeguards the lower back. As you breathe in, feel the sides of your rib cage widening.

151
Keep on the move
After comparing back pain studies worldwide, the Royal College of Physicians' Faculty of Occupational Medicine states that only 5 per cent of sufferers benefit from time off work, as being in bed can worsen lower back pain. Break from your work station once an hour to walk around or try one of the exercises here.

152
Heat-wrap your back
To ease tight muscles while you work, try propping a heat pack or hot water bottle against the lower back support on your chair. Researchers at Johns Hopkins University School of Medicine found heat packs helped workers get back to tasks quicker.

153
Exercise the pain away
Gentle exercise seems to be the one surefire way to combat lower back pain. Look for classes that focus on muscle-strengthening and gentle stretching and include an element of relaxation. Then start gently, gradually building up in intensity. In a study at Hull University's Institute of Rehabilitation, patients who took just eight classes were in less pain and more able to control their back problems a year later.

Enrol in a yoga class and learn how to protect your lower back.

154
Find a lunchtime yoga class

A study reported in *Annals of Internal Medicine* found that yoga was more effective for lower back pain than other general exercise classes. Look for classes in remedial and Iyengar yoga, which suit those with health issues.

155
Try t'ai chi

If lower back pain seems to be linked to stiff hips, look for a lunchtime t'ai chi class. In t'ai chi, you learn a sequence of slow, continuous movements that focus on fluidity and teach you to engage your mind in every action. This promotes greater mobility in the joints, lowers blood pressure, boosts the immune system and raises energy, ensuring that afternoons feel less pressured.

156
Figure-of-eight exercise

This shape is considered a powerful way to bring together dissipated energy – in homeopathy, it's used to potentize tinctures. This exercise keeps the hips mobile and, as it requires balance and co-ordination, focuses the mind. Standing with feet hip-width apart, take your weight to the right foot. Raise the left foot (hold a wall for stability) and make a figure-of-eight motion: swing the leg forwards for the top loop and behind for the bottom one. Start with small movements, gradually making them larger and faster. Repeat on the other side.

157
Broadening the sacrum

Lying on your back, bend up your knees and draw your heels comfortably close to your buttocks, keeping your feet hip-width apart. Feel the back of your pelvic bone against the floor. Let both knees fall to the right a few inches and then to the left, just enough to feel the weight roll from one side of the sacrum to the other. Repeat the sequence about 20 times until you feel the lower back release.

158
Flank stretch

Lie on your back with your knees bent up and your feet flat on the floor, then cross your right ankle over to rest on top of your left thigh. Hold the back of your left knee (if this is tricky, thread a belt or scarf around the back of the knee to hold on to), then slowly draw both legs towards your chest. Change legs and repeat the exercise.

159
Child pose

Kneeling in front of a chair, place your big toes together and then widen your knees. Sit back down on your heels (on a cushion if this is more comfortable) and rest forwards, relaxing onto the seat of the chair. Try to keep the shins in contact with the floor. If this feels easy, move the chair forwards until your spine lengthens, or dispense with the chair altogether and rest your head on the floor.

160

Opening breath

Practise this with a partner, swapping roles. Kneel, then sit your buttocks down on your heels, widen your knees and drop your head down to the floor, taking your arms by your sides, the palms facing upwards. Feel free to place a supportive cushion beneath your hips or head. Ask your partner to kneel behind you and gently rest his hands on the middle of your back. Breathe slowly into the hands then ask him to move his hands to the side of your ribs and feel your breath here, expanding sideways. Finally, ask him to move his hands to the upper back region and then breathe slowly and deeply again. Allow yourself time to understand that the breath moves the back of the body as well as the front. This not only frees the spine but can be extremely calming.

161

Homeopathy for back pain

Try the following remedies:
• Aesculus 30 for acute pain in the lumbo-sacral region that makes it hard to stand upright. Pains are hot and needle-like and worse when bending.
• Bryonia 30 for pain of the lumbar area made worse by movement. Also for stiffness in the small of the back relieved by pressure or the support of tight clothing.
• Cimicifuga 30 for pain in the lumbar region that extends to the hips and thighs during menstruation.

162

Table release

This is an astonishingly effective exercise, providing a pleasing stretch to the calf muscles as well as being extremely relaxing for the lower back.

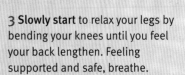

1 Snug your thighs against a table, then step back until you can straighten your legs at an angle behind you, toes tucked under.

2 Lie the whole of your body flat on the table, turning your head to the side to rest your cheek on your hands. Keep the stretch in the legs.

3 Slowly start to relax your legs by bending your knees until you feel your back lengthen. Feeling supported and safe, breathe.

Dealing with deadlines

Constantly working to deadlines seriously raises stress, shows research, prompting blood pressure, respiration and heart rate to rise as stress hormones surge through your system. In the short term, this leaves you wiped out; in the long term, it leads to heart disease, stroke and depression. Use these strategies to cope with excessive demands.

163

Above all eat

Eating regular meals is a proven stress-reduction technique, equipping body and mind to cope with panic conditions.

164

Eat by colour

Stress hormones, such as cortisol, deplete the body of the essential vitamins it needs to maintain health and wellbeing. During times of tension, build your diet around dark green, yellow and red fruit and vegetables, which top up your

Opt for brightly coloured fresh fruit and vegetables to strengthen immunity.

vitamin content (drizzle with extra-virgin olive oil to aid absorption). The antioxidant carotenoids that bring about the vibrant colours also boost your immunity and protect the body against heart disease.

165

Avoid foods linked to stress

The following foods increase and maintain levels of stress hormones, so avoid during deadline periods: high-fat processed foods, sugary snacks, alcohol, caffeinated drinks.

166

Up your protein

Amino acids can alter chemicals in the brain to increase energy, counter anxiety, stabilize moods and reduce cravings. At times of stress, try to eat protein (the source of amino acids) at each meal. The best sources are meat, fish and eggs, or combine plant proteins, like rice and beans.

167
Yummy yogurt
Enjoy a small pot of rich, creamy natural or bio yogurt (stir in runny manuka honey) if deadlines upset your digestion. Swedish research suggests that workers who eat yogurt daily take fewer days off sick.

168
Drink pomegranate juice
Sip pomegranate juice for its antioxidant polyphenols that help to zap stress-induced free radicals and protect the heart. It also relieves nervous tummies. Add a squeeze of lime for extra zing.

169
Don't skip your workout
No matter how vital the deadline, don't let it interfere with a regular yoga class or gym session. Exercise keeps you feeling relaxed and productive as well as countering long-term stress-related ailments, from depression to heart disease. Inscribe workouts into your diary (call them appointments if you must) and treat them as sacrosanct.

170
Take a nap
A snooze during the day can work wonders for productivity, found researchers tracking a group of

Enjoy the heart-protecting qualities of naturally sweet pomegranate juice.

workers who napped for around 30 minutes three times a week at midday. It also helped this group of men cut their risk of heart problems by more than a third.

171
Burn focusing oils
Add 2–4 drops of one of the following essential oils to a room vaporizer to help balance the mind:
• Basil focuses the mind and senses, and calms the nerves.
• Black pepper strengthens the nerves and promotes stamina.
• Bergamot relieves anxiety and cools anger.
• Frankincense soothes the mind and comforts.
• Geranium destresses and helps to lift the spirits.

172
Keep essences to hand
Reach for a Bach Flower Essence when you feel over-burdened. Place 4 drops in a glass of water and sip until symptoms subside. In extreme cases, place directly on your tongue.
• Centaury if you find it hard to say no and are put upon by colleagues.
• Elm if you take on too much and feel burdened by responsibility.

173
Coffee replacement
The homeopathic remedy Coffea 30, made from coffee beans, heals the symptoms linked to coffee: a mental rush, racing heart and sense of excitement followed by tiredness.

174
Pressure drop remedy
In high-pressure times, try Kali. Phos tissue salts. This low-potency homeopathic remedy supports the nervous system during nervous exhaustion or emotional strain. Take frequent doses of 2 tablets up to four times daily if you are very tired or having a tough day.

175
Get a life!
Relishing a life outside work helps employees cope with demanding positions. If you have an activity to

A brisk power walk each day helps to revitalize both body and mind.

get to in the evening, you are more likely to retain a well-balanced, relaxed outlook on work problems.

176

Flee outdoors

Infrequent breaks are a key cause of stress and injury at work. The Health and Safety Executive suggests a 5–10 minute break after each hour of keyboard or monitor work. This is more relaxing than saving up the minutes for a long break. Get out to bask in the sun, breathe in fresh air or walk briskly around the block.

177

Schedule downtime

When you have to reach a deadline, build in sanity-saving treats and rest times. This might be a dash to the sandwich bar, or going out for a run.

178

Be a buddy

Keeping on good terms with co-workers keeps down pressure in the workplace. A 2003 study found that people who muck in together are more productive, perhaps because they read indirect communication cues well. Another study found that people with work buddies had lowered blood-pressure readings in stressful work situations. Invite co-workers for a drink after work, or treat everyone to ice cream.

179
Smile
If you feel like crying, smile. Studies show that acting happy triggers the biochemical changes that result in happiness, just as people asked to act anxiously saw the same physical changes as those who were anxious.

180
Cross-patterning
Stand up and lift your right arm and left leg, touching your left knee with your right hand. Repeat on the other side, then continue, building up a smooth, flowing action. This helps to connect both hemispheres of the brain, restoring focus and energy.

181
When it's all too much
Head to the toilet. Stand with feet hip-width apart, pivot forwards and hang, holding opposite elbows. Relax your neck and upper body. This brings freshly oxygenated blood to the upper body. After a minute, come up slowly, stacking vertebrae one on the other. Bring up your head last. (Avoid with high blood pressure.)

182
Undoing knots meditation
Sit comfortably with your back straight and arms relaxed. Close your eyes and observe your

Restore focus with this brain-connecting cross-patterning exercise.

breathing. When you feel calmer, imagine your cares as a bunch of strings that have tangled into knots. Some strings might be attached to work projects, others to children and partners. Imagine unpicking the knots. As they loosen, feel your troubles straightening out and see how unravelling a few knots loosens others. After 10–20 minutes, grow aware of your surroundings before opening your eyes.

183
Look for challenges
A little stress is welcome as it brings motivating adrenalin. It may also boost the immune system, suggests research from the University of Kentucky and the University of British Columbia, but only if the challenge is defined, attainable and has an end date, after which you can relax. Seek short-term challenges to boost self-esteem: volunteer to give a presentation or make a tricky call. Just be sure to relax afterwards.

184
Spot the warning signs
If the following symptoms result from work pressure, talk to your doctor and manager and keep a "triggers and symptoms" diary:
- insomnia
- headaches
- digestive complaints
- loss of concentration
- short temper
- anxiety and depression

Time-management tips

Trying to shoehorn too many tasks into too few hours – especially if you have limited control over the tasks – is a major source of stress at work. In a poll of United Kingdom employees by the Trades Union Congress, 74 per cent attributed workplace stress to overload. Cultivate essential coping skills, starting by analysing your time management: assess your priorities to use the time to your best advantage.

185
No more Monday mornings

By planning your time well, you rid yourself of Monday-morning dread and empower yourself to make difficult decisions and tackle off-putting tasks. You may also find you counter the new workplace stressor, digital overload. Vow to start today.

186
Getting real

Until you know how you use your time, it's tricky to know how to handle it more efficiently. So for one full week before starting a task estimate how long it will take. After completing it, record the exact timing. At the end of the week, compare the two figures. Indicate discrepancies with a highlighter pen

Keep stimulated by planning a mix of tasks throughout the day.

and identify your major time-eaters. What steps can you take to ameliorate matters?

187
Confide in someone

Confiding that you feel time-stressed can help overcome the problem. Even if you don't find solutions, the act of voicing fears begins the process of taking them seriously enough to find solutions.

188
Work that diary

Block out tasks in your diary with appropriate timings. Try to book in a mix of activities to stay focused: wall-to-wall meetings or interviews fry your brain. Book times to eat, rest and exercise. It helps to divide the day into blocks: for silent focus, meetings, calls and emailing.

189
Right task, right time

Work out what works best for you: if you focus better in the morning, do detailed work then and plan meetings and calls after lunch.

190
Use lists

Writing down tasks crystallizes them. Make three lists. List A comprises short-term tasks that can be achieved in a day; list B, tasks that can be achieved in a week, and list C, items that might take a month to complete. Order the tasks on each list in terms of priority. Start and end each day by reviewing your lists, striking off tasks from list A and shifting priorities over from list B. Each week complete something towards a task from list C. On Friday afternoon, order Monday's list A.

191
Step back
Every so often, step back to ask yourself if you're following your plan for the day, and doing the most useful task for that time. Could anyone else do it more usefully?

192
Think positive
Frame tasks in a positive way to process work speedily. Think "This is a new challenge" rather than "I've never done anything like this before". Focusing on how hard a task is slows you down.

193
Delegating
Give people the benefit of the doubt. If you ask them to do something, many will rise to the occasion and feel more valued for it. Ask co-workers what you could do for each other to destress each other's roles. Have a no-holds-barred session to work out ways to tackle each person's problems.

194
Act like a Roman
If you have control over where you do business, act like the Romans and hold meetings out of the office in rejuvenating locations. The Romans favoured the bathhouse: their version of the spa and gym.

195
Use every minute
Rather than putting off a task because you don't have a long run of hours in which to complete it, start it now, and run at it in any time you have free. In five minutes of real focus much can be achieved.

196
Reclaim dead time
Use dead time between meetings, while waiting for the kettle to boil or a document to print to make a call, reply to an email, review notes or strike off other short-term tasks.

197
Hire the best
When hiring staff, make it your aim to take on people who are better than you. Then stop worrying and delegate responsibility.

198
Grasp the nettle
Don't move scary tasks down the list. Anticipation only makes them scarier and adds worry time. Tackle important, scary things quickly and while you feel fresh; reserve coasting tasks for the "pm slump".

199
Don't be a technology slave
To engineer a run of uninterrupted peace, turn off the phone for an hour and just check emails once an hour. Even better, check only twice a day, responding to urgent ones. A study of Microsoft workers found that after replying to an email, they took about 15 minutes to get back on track.

200
No-email day
One day each week encourage colleagues to talk face to face or on the phone rather than send emails.

201
Multi-tasking switch-off
Many of us multi-task mercilessly to process work, but this may be causing us extra stress suggests a 2006 report in the journal *Neuron*. It showed that multi-tasking increases the risk of mistakes and slows down your efficiency rate by disrupting the ability to process information.

202
Shut the door

If your office is besieged by people, shut the door for a set time each day and make sure people know they can't disturb you. Let colleagues know your "surgery" hours.

203
Escape from meetings

Why not hold a meeting to see if all your meetings are necessary? Could some decisions be made using email attachments or conference calls?

204
Do say no

Value yourself and your time enough to say no to people and tasks when your diary is full.

205
Stand up

Instead of sitting for informal meetings, stand up. This encourages everyone to spit out what they need to say and then get back to work.

206
Use your in-tray

Don't pile up stuff, use your in-tray as an in-tray. When work comes in, prioritize it, then take it out of the tray to complete it before shifting it into someone else's in-tray.

207
Stop procrastinating

Rather than agonize about a task – which wastes time – just do it. Act on mail as you open it, rely on instincts and step up to decision-making. You then free up time and stop stressing about being stressed.

208
Detox your office

"Desk stress" is management speak for a cluttered office. It creates extra stress, reminding you of jobs not yet done. Take a few precious minutes to file papers you are not working on – and see how much you can bin.

209
Nobody's perfect

Lower your expectations if time is tight. Perfectionists may put things off through fear of not producing a stunning result. Aim to be good enough: your good enough may be someone else's A-grade.

210
Concentration point

If your energy is zapped by the very thought of your work load, keep a concentration focus to tether your mind to: maybe a rose, a pebble or a spiritual object. A single focus encourages steadiness and control. **Examine the object**, fixing it in your mind in three dimensions. Look at colour, shape and texture and think of the qualities it embodies, perhaps perfection, solidity or compassion. **Close your eyes.** Visualize the image in an intense light between your eyes. Focus on its qualities. If it's a rose, for example, feel its essence with your senses: its scent, thin petals, its sap. **If your mind drifts,** redirect it back to the object. After meditating, sit quietly for a few minutes before beginning work.

211

Knowing when to go home

People with a good social and family life seem to be inoculated against the negative effects of stress, but this doesn't happen if you don't devote time to it. Decide a cut-off point at which you leave work to exercise, pick up children or get the train. Don't let anyone eat into this time. If necessary, start early the next day to deal with yesterday's excess.

212

Revisit your working week

Can you work three long days, or work a day at home to reduce rush-hour commutes and office politics?

213

Ask for help

Make enquiries about whether your workplace or a professional body offers courses in time management, delegating, negotiating or setting goals at work. Professional face-to-face help always beats advice from a book or website.

214

Think on this

Pin up this statement by the 19th-century Indian sage Sri Ramakrishna: "The mind of a yogi is under his control; he is not under the control of his mind.'"

A tidy office is destressing and focuses your mind on the job at hand.

Career audit

Studies suggest that the jobs most harmful to our physical and psychological wellbeing are very demanding ones over which we have little control. In such jobs – where demands are never met – the body's stress response is not antidoted by a feeling of satisfaction, and physical and mental health, as well as job satisfaction, suffer. If this describes you, it might be time to look at more healthy employment options.

215
Reclaim meaning

Routine tasks that have little apparent meaning are considered significant job stressors by America's National Institute for Occupational Safety and Health. If you think that the work you are doing doesn't utilize your skills fully, look for another outlet for your creativity and initiative – take an online writing course perhaps, or rebuild a classic car after hours – and raise the issue of job satisfaction at your next performance review.

216
Reality check

Do any of the things that stress you at work right now really matter? Stop fussing for two minutes and ask yourself if they will be significant in six months, one year and five years. If so, maybe you should plan to do something about them. If not, stop worrying and take the long view.

217
Assess your stress

List your work stressors: endless meetings, computer systems, some colleagues? Beside each one write down how, in a blue-sky world, you could resolve them. Mull it over.

218
Look at your job description

Dig out your job description. Does it still define your role, or have expectations changed? Might this be a source of stress? Use performance reviews to pinpoint things that need to change. You might need to upgrade your skills, hire an assistant or look for promotion.

219
Are you in the right job?

Do your characteristics match your job description? What is stressful to one person might be a buzz for another. Your stress may result from

Think about where you are heading and don't be afraid to aim high.

being in the wrong role. In one column, list your characteristics that affect your work, plus your coping style and training. In another column jot down your tasks. Try to draw lines between the two. Are you a good match? Could you be with training? Does your job need a redesign? Do family matters interfere with work or vice versa? Assess whether you should retrain or pursue a new path.

220
Find a role model

Is there someone at work whose success and skills you admire? Try to find out where he or she trained and what makes them tick. Could you ask someone to be your mentor?

221
Do you have a career path?

To relax at work it's good to have a sense of direction. Feeling that your potential isn't recognized is a key source of stress. Do you need to talk to your manager about the future?

222
Write your future

Think back to you aged eight. What did you think you'd be doing now? Write down those expectations. Pick out words that still appeal. Repeat the exercise, thinking back to you aged 16. Could you change anything to build in some of those words?

223
Set your goals

Write down where you want to be at the end of your career. What do you need to have achieved in the next five or 10 years to get there? What steps do you need to take in the next 12 months? Make a monthly plan of action: include time for research, time to accrue savings, make applications or hand in your resignation. Review your plan on the first day of each month.

224
Fill out questionnaires

Try online career assessments that appraise your motivation, talents, temperament and aptitude for different careers, and suggest routes for acquiring skills and training.

225
Have a baby

If you've hit 30 and are in a loving relationship, why not throw caution to the wind? Pregnancy is a perfect excuse to recast your life as it forces you to confront work-life options. Even not working for a while.

226
Shopping around

Look for employers with family-friendly working options, policies to combat stress and opportunities to

Online questionnaires highlight skills, helping you to assess your career and perhaps consider a change of direction.

develop. Studies show that supportive workplaces make a real difference in reducing stress, even if work loads are high. What makes a difference is engaged supervisors and supportive co-workers.

227
United we stand

Join a union. There's only so much you can do as an individual about a workplace culture that causes stress in its employees. As a group, you can join a wider campaign for decent working conditions, a reduction in working hours and disciplining bullying bosses. Long-established unions have plenty of experience and often make breakthroughs that smaller workplace-based organizations struggle with.

Zapping work rage

In one survey, 64 per cent of people had experienced "office rage". Anger causes heart and breathing rates and blood pressure to increase, muscles to tense, the immune response to shut down and the digestive system to suffer. Frequent anger increases the risk of high blood pressure, heart disease and diabetes. Fortunately, risk is minimized if you learn to avoid, defuse and address situations that make you feel angry.

228
Pinpoint the source
If anger becomes a habitual response to stressful situations, try to distinguish between the triggers and underlying sources of your anger. For example, when someone turns into the parking space at work you thought was yours, he or she triggers your anger, but probably isn't its actual source. Being aware of this distinction can help you step back from heated emotions.

229
Look back in anger
In order to identify the real source of your rage, think about how angry and frustrating incidents really make you feel – perhaps unsupported, afraid or guilty? It can help to relate these feelings to episodes of anger that occurred during your childhood and the emotions that underpinned or fed into your reactions at that time.

230
Learn to let go
Repeatedly replaying a stressful scenario in your mind may result in ill health, so try to switch off and stop thinking about the event in question. In a study, reflecting on a past event that caused anger or upset was found to suppress the body's levels of immunoglobulin A for as much as six hours: these antibodies are the frontline troops that help to protect your body from infection and disease.

Clary sage helps you to gain perspective on worries.

231
Avoidance tactics
Avoid irritating situations or people. Keep a triggers diary to help you gauge irritants, then look at how you can rearrange the day to avoid them.

232
Seek out good things
Finding positive situations and people bubble-wraps you from the bad stuff. Think positively to boost psychological and physical health.

233
Use destressing techniques
When you simply can't avoid a stressy situation, use supportive strategies to help you survive, such

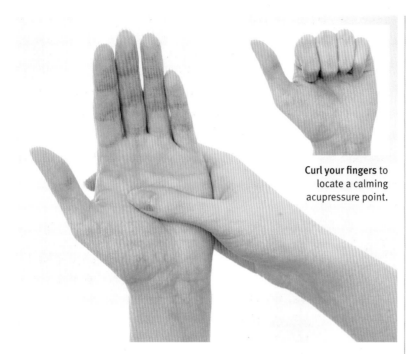

Curl your fingers to locate a calming acupressure point.

Apply firm pressure to help destress.

as homeopathic remedies, aromatherapy, exercise and meditation. Try to eat healthily, drink plenty of water, get sufficient sleep and make time for the loved ones who support you.

234
Feed your brain
In order to be able to react in a sane way to inflammatory situations, it helps to have a clear head. Omega-3 fats keep the brain's neural transmitters functioning to keep us calm and tuned-in, yet most of us eat fewer than is healthy. Aim to eat oily fish (such as mackerel and sardines) at least twice a week, and snack on a handful of walnuts daily.

235
Don't reach for cake
Stress hormones bring about a drop in levels of serotonin, the hormone that calms. Carbohydrates boost the body's serotonin levels, which is why we crave cake and stodge at times of stress. Try to keep carb cravings in check by eating porridge for breakfast and snacking on oat cakes in the day. When you eat bread, make sure it's wholemeal.

236
Burn calming oils
Add 2–4 drops of one of the following relaxing essential oils to a room vaporizer:

- Bergamot quells anger.
- Clary sage eases panic and puts things into perspective.
- Juniper cleanses the atmosphere.
- Lemon helps to refresh and clear a troubled mind.

237
Light incense
Sandalwood incense is recommended to bring peace and soothe states of nervous anxiety and tension in a room. It is thought to soften entrenched attitudes and allow people to move on.

238
Calming pressure point
Tightly shut the fingers of your left hand. The point beneath the tip of your middle finger is a powerfully calming acupressure point. Release tension by exerting pressure onto this point with the tip of your right thumb for one minute.

239
Cooling breath
When you feel so angry that you become flushed and sweaty, stick out your tongue and roll up the sides to form a tube (some people simply can't do this, so don't get stressed if that includes you). Breathe in slowly and deeply through the tube and then exhale slowly through your nose.

Divert anger: channel your energies into learning an engrossing new skill.

240
Controlling breath
Sit upright (on the floor or a chair) and start to focus on your breathing, listening to the sound of your breath and noticing your breathing pattern. Count the length of each inhalation and exhalation. See if you can make both the same length. Don't force the breath to change; allow it to happen gradually. Finally, at the end of each exhalation, try to hold your breath, gently building up to the same length of time as the breaths: for example, breathe in for four, out for four and hold for four. Practise this for as long as it feels easy, then return to regular breathing.

241
Count to 10
Before blurting out angry words – that you could regret later – take a breath and count to 10. If, after this, you still feel like saying them, go ahead. Giving yourself space to think allows you to express your point of view in a more measured and productive way.

242
Cry it out
The body rids itself of stress hormones through tears, so if anger just makes you want to weep, then feel free and go ahead.

243
Remedies to ease anger
• Nux.Vom 30 is ideal for people with an irritable or fiery temperament who like to take action and get things done and get wound up easily by anything they perceive as an obstacle.
• Sepia 30 is the remedy for women whose sudden bursts of impatience and manic busyness usually occur pre-menstrually.

244
Ayurvedic solutions
The ancient Indian art of healthcare, Ayurveda, regards anger as an excess of *pitta*, one of three energies in the body. To reduce *pitta*, avoid spicy or sour foods and take cool showers. If you practise yoga, steer clear of inversions and sun salutations.

245
Just shut up
To stop work rage in its tracks, stop talking, walk to a window and simply stare out for a few minutes. Do nothing but observe your breath moving in and out. Follow a cloud or plane across the sky. Do this for a full five minutes.

246
Punch it out
If you are naturally hot-tempered, seek out leisure pursuits at lunchtime and after work that help

you diffuse some of your tension before returning home. In kickboxing classes, you learn safe techniques for punching and kicking that allow you to channel your aggression and gain a sense of achievement. The system also hones co-ordination and balance, which promotes equilibrium.

247
Run on a treadmill

Jogging on a treadmill for 30 minutes has a calming, sedative effect on overheated emotions – and people with honed muscles seem to shrug off stress better than those who don't train, according to a study reported in the *American Journal of Hypertension.*

248
Fly trapeze

Learning a completely new skill that requires total concentration is an ideal way to diffuse anger if you feel frustrated in your work life. And a skill that stops people in their tracks, such as trapeze-flying or tightrope-walking, brings a powerful boost to your self-esteem. Take weekly lessons at a circus skills' school to diffuse physical and emotional tension and quickly build up core strength.

249
Accepting change

Life (and work) is a process of constant and inevitable change – if you try to battle against this, you will inevitably face dissatisfaction, disappointment and struggle. Try cultivating a detachment that allows you to react in a more measured way when conditions mutate, people let you down and technology malfunctions. If you expect the unknown to disrupt well-laid plans, you become better able to accept change without resentment – and so remain open to new options.

250
Think like a woman

In an influential study, people who adopted traditionally "female" ways of dealing with stressful events and situations – befriending and nurturing – stayed healthier than

people who adopted traditionally "male" strategies – withdrawing and acting hostile.

251
Inner smile

Sit comfortably upright, close your eyes and focus on your breathing. Once calm, imagine an inner smile. Let it light up your toes and pass up your legs and pelvis, your abdomen, back, chest, arms, hands, shoulders and neck, your face and head. As the smile reaches an area, feel your muscles relax and a sense of lightness. Retain this lightness and inner smile as you step back into the world.

252
Buy a Buddha

Place a Buddha on your desk to remind you of your inner smile.

253
Stay united

Bad working conditions are a key source of stress, suggests research. If your office rage is caused by bad workplace conditions – old equipment, cramped space, noise or air pollution – meet with colleagues and a union representative to decide what should change. Talking to superiors en masse can have impact.

Be Buddha-like: stay calm and embrace your inner smile.

Working from home

Wipe out "work miles" – those unproductive, deeply unrelaxing journeys to your workspace – and office politics by setting up a home office. This can allow you to spend more time with your family and to organize your day to suit your lifestyle and personality: perhaps you do your best work late at night or very early in the morning, for example, and so can liberate more daylight hours for positive, relaxing activities. Well, that's the idea!

holidays and less uninterrupted headspace. Find out about the stresses of home working and the resources you require to make it a success by talking candidly to those who already work this way.

254
Avoiding extra stress
Working for yourself from home may sound ideal, but for many of us it results in longer hours, fewer

255
Making it work
Successful home workers tend to be self-starters who can monitor their work, set deadlines, make decisions and ignore distractions. They enjoy their own company and can switch off from work at the end of the day. If this doesn't describe you at core (some of these skills can be learned), think carefully about home working.

Claim your space and close the door to the rest of the household.

256
Relax behind a door

Many people find it helps to work in a space that they can close the door on, shutting themselves off from household concerns and harnessing their mind to work matters. Think hard if your home workspace is a corner of the kitchen table.

257
Book a meeting space

If you feel uneasy putting your house on show to clients, book meeting spaces outside the home – either informally in a café or in serviced space within a business park or hotel.

258
Peaceful places to work

If your home is tiny, look at installing an outdoor workspace. It is destressing to close the door on the home and open the door of your private office world. A basic shed can be bought relatively cheaply for self-assembly and might not need planning permission. Bespoke wooden garden buildings or former railway carriages kitted out with insulation and heating are more expensive. Alternatively, look to hire a space with a like-minded group of individuals to share the cost of equipment such as fridge, photocopier and coffee machine.

259
Setting parameters

Vow to start work and finish work at set times, and resist the temptation to sneak a look at emails when you should be with your partner or kids.

260
Avoiding interruption

Discourage neighbours and friends from interrupting by not answering the door unless someone has an appointment. Make sure they know the times when you are available to have a gossip.

261
Buying in help

If you can't concentrate because a mountain of washing up calls or you can't reach your outdoor work oasis for brambles, call a house meeting and distribute tasks or hire a cleaner or gardener. For workspaces, cleaners can be tax-deductible.

262
Beating procrastination

This is more of a mind-stress at home as there are so many more chores to distract you. If you have trouble starting work, list the reasons why on paper. On the other side say why they are not legitimate concerns. Or break a task into parts and begin with the most enjoyable one.

Mix essential oils to create an invigorating room spray.

263
Enhance your brain waves

Play music to set the relaxed but productive tone of your home office. You may gain in concentration from working to a Bach fugue or from the modern minimalism of La Mont Young's pieces.

264
Relaxing room spray

In a plant-spray bottle, add 5 drops of essential oil to every 10ml of spring water and spritz your workspace when you can't focus on the task in hand:
- To revive flagging spirits: bergamot, lemongrass.
- To restore balance: melissa.
- To energize: peppermint, rosemary.
- To boost inspiration and creativity: ginger.

2 Relax at home

To safeguard your wellbeing and counter the effects of stress at work, it's essential to be able to chill out at home. Restoring work-life balance is key now technology such as the mobile phone, email and Blackberry lets work intrude into home time. Clutter is another modern stressor. As we accumulate stuff so we are constantly reminded of tidying to be done and uncompleted tasks. Guilt and low-grade stress then grow, stopping us from relaxing and making stress-related conditions more likely. Here are ways to dissolve this anxiety, from tips to create a relaxing home to fulfilling pastimes. When your home is uncluttered and filled with objects, people and activities you love, you feel nurtured and can relax and recharge.

Home sanctuary

If your home feels like a refuge, once you step over the threshold you shed work stresses and benefit your mental and physical wellbeing. Human behaviour is influenced by its environment, and a welcoming space starts the relaxation response. Hospital studies show that natural light, a view of nature, uplifting art and green-tinted walls reduce the need for pain medication and can cut a stay by days. Here are tips to give your own space such nurturing properties.

Adorn your door with flowers and plants.

265
Want to spend time at home
For home to be a haven, you have to want to be there. If you feel the need to go out a lot, ask why. Record your childhood memories of home. Returning from school is a good prompt. Fix on physical or sensual memories, such as the look of your door, the smell that greeted you and the sounds you heard on opening the door. What clues does this give you about your current home?

266
Beautify your threshold
The entrance to a house marks the transition between outside and inside, public and private, interior and material worlds. The Indian art of placement, *vaastu shastra*, considers it one of a home's most charged energy sites. Afford it respect: paint the door a beautiful colour and grow plants either side.

267
Raise herbs by a door
Keeping pots of scented herbs with soothing or uplifting properties, such as lavender, rosemary, mint and lemon verbena, by a door allows you to brush them with your hand as you pass to release the fragrant oils.

268
Renew the door
In India, it is thought that the energy patterns and karma of past lives disturb the harmony of the present. By replacing the front door every three generations, the ghosts of the past are brushed away, and

Amethyst has restorative properties.

fresh energy ushered in. As lives change and trends move on, refresh your door to replenish your reserves of relaxed good energy.

269
Techno-phobes unite
Technology invades more and more of the home, from television screens at the end of the bed and in the fridge door to computers always left on. Keep some rooms free from electronic equipment: some natural therapists believe electromagnetic fields sap energy and hinder relaxation. Keep one silent space to retreat to and daydream, read or nap. Dare to get rid of the television!

270
Make a creative space
To truly relax we need an outlet for our creativity. Try to set aside some space at home to tempt you away

from the television and sofa: convert an attic into an artist's studio, a basement into a photographic dark room or set up an easel in front of the bedroom window.

271
Crystal healing

Place crystal citrine (also known as Cairngorm) in a room. Its warming and comforting properties help to cleanse and protect the surrounding environment from any negative energies. Add amethyst to promote ease and restfulness.

272
Matching moods

Bright colours stimulate the emotions, mind and energy levels, while more muted hues are relaxing, helping you to unwind. So reserve stimulating shades of yellow for offices and workrooms, and avoid intense or clashing combinations, which can be over-stimulating. Nurture the kitchen and the bedroom with hearty reds and enriching oranges, colours that encourage warmth and sociable relationships. Use calming, soothing blues and greens, which are proven to reduce blood pressure, for relaxing, laid-back living rooms.

273
Relaxing colour schemes

Research in hospitals shows that being surrounded by green or views of a garden speeds the healing process. Colour therapists value green for its rebalancing and nurturing qualities, and its calming effect on over-wrought emotions. Experiment with light shades of green in a living space.

Create a tranquil retreat with the colours of nature and plenty of natural light.

274
Colour for minimalists
If you're a confirmed minimalist and veer away from colour, experiment tentatively by introducing calming hues in the form of throws and cushions, rugs and paintings.

275
Hang uplifting art
San Diego hospital patients treated in rooms with uplifting art reported positive effects, and patients in a Pennsylvania hospital surrounded by art and flowers recovered more quickly and needed less narcotics and nursing care than those with a view of a brick wall. Fill your walls with spirit-nourishing objects.

276
Instant freshen-up
Open a window for a blast of fresh air (air inside is two to five times more polluted than outdoor air).

277
Contemplate nature photos
In a 2002 study, post-operative patients who contemplated nature photographs felt less anxious than those who looked at a blank panel,

Keep windows spotless to maximize natural lighting.

computer-generated art or nothing. Colour photographs were especially calming. Try the effects for yourself.

278
Seasonal perfuming
Nature promotes calmness. In spring, cultivate hyacinths or paper whites indoors to create a heavenly perfume. In summer, bring in vases of roses, lilac and honeysuckle. Make winter pomanders by puncturing oranges with cloves.

279
Background sounds
In Indian music, the veena, a fine stringed instrument, trains listeners to be attentive because of its delicate

Bring the outside in with a vase of freshly cut, scented flowers.

sound. As you listen, you train your hearing to perceive the peace of nothingness. Achieve this effect with modern classical music turned low. Try Steve Reich, Eric Satie or Brian Eno's *Discreet Music*, composed to be played in the background.

280

Let in the light

Replace bulky curtains with blinds and remove nets to maximize the amount of natural light. This boosts wellbeing and clarity of thought: in studies, students got higher scores when tested in naturally lit rooms.

281

Find a window cleaner

Cleaning windows once a month inside and out makes a surprising difference to the amount of light that gets through. Make it a priority.

282

Relax the lighting

Avoid overhead lights (take out the bulbs to stop you using them). Opt for ambient spotlights and lamps to create cosy corners to relax in.

283

Space-clearing sprays

Try homeopathic space-clearing room sprays that contain Bach Flower Essences, which can make rooms smell beautifully fresh and help to address emotional or energetic blockages.

284

Incense for day and night

Look for Japanese incense designed for different times of day: wake-up blends for the bathroom as you prepare for work and wind-down combinations for a sleepy bedroom.

285

Relaxing outdoors

If you have outdoor space, create inviting areas to relax, eat or share a drink. Angle seating to catch the sun: a table and chairs for breakfast, a shady arbour for midday dining or a summerhouse for cool afternoons.

286

Calming planting

Cultivate plants with relaxing properties: maybe a bed of aromatic herbs, such as lavender, rosemary and lemon verbena with scented roses. For serene sounds, try bamboo or a tinkling fountain. Grow camomile between paving slabs: it emits a calming scent when trodden on. For a peaceful evening garden, opt for plants like jasmine that give off scent as the light fades.

287

Outdoor vibes

Let music enhance the vibe. Joni Mitchell plays well on hot days or try the deep roots reggae of U Roy, Johnny Clarke or Augustus Pablo.

Transform your garden into a calm oasis with well-placed seating and enticing aromas.

Home meditation zone

If you go to a weekly yoga or meditation class, carrying through your resolution to practise at home helps to lighten the guilt you can feel before lessons. The best way to boost motivation is to dedicate a small space at home to your practice. Follow the suggestions here to transform the space into a serene and tranquil place of retreat.

Gently focusing on a geometric pattern can restore order to a busy mind and harness the emotions.

288

Make a home yoga space

Clear a cluttered corner of a bedroom or take over a rarely used dining room, make space in a garden shed or, in summer, find a sheltered spot outdoors. The ideal spot will be well ventilated, but warm enough when you are sitting still or lying motionless. Make sure you have enough room to lay out a sticky mat, spread your arms and legs wide and stretch upwards. A clear wall would be useful. Then remove unnecessary furniture and sweep the floor. Brushing in an outwards direction is said to rid a room of negative vibes.

289

Ideal site

The Indian art of *vaastu shastra* says that the ideal site for a yoga and meditation space is in the north-east part of a home. Here, energy is said to be light and brilliant and a source of spiritual nourishment. A site down a few steps would be ideal,

since a space lower than the rest of the plot collects and channels positive energy. Keep the space open and uncluttered by positioning furniture to the sides of the room.

290

Ayurvedic colours

Decorate your contemplation space in white, gold, violet or blue – *sattwic* colours that engender joy, harmony, peace, serenity and contemplative thoughts. Avoid muddy brown and black or greys, considered *tamasic*: causing the mind to become stale and inert.

291

Yoga essentials

Stack yoga blocks in your space with a yoga belt and a couple of solid cushions or bolsters to allow you to achieve poses with comfort. Add a blanket or shawl to cover you in the final relaxation pose. You might like a towel to wipe away sweat. Invest in a thicker, heavyweight

mat if you have a permanent home-practice space. These tend to be wider and longer than regular sticky yoga mats, so more of your body stays cushioned when you stretch from fingertips to toes. They permit a very relaxing *Savasana* relaxation at the end of a session.

292

Pre-yoga shower

Wash away the stress of the day before you start your practice. If you have less time, simply wash your hands, feet and face.

2 tbsp unscented shower gel
6 drops essential oil of sandalwood
2 drops essential oil of patchouli

Combine the gel and oils, then use this to wash with in the shower or bath or pour beneath running taps for a bubble bath.

293
Mandala meditation

Hang a mandala on the wall, level with your eyes when seated. These geometric designs rebalance the mind (which is drawn to order) and emotions to bring about the relaxation response. Either start at the outer edge of the circle and let your eyes wander inwards, or find the central focal point and let your gaze move out. Gaze softly at the mandala; don't focus intently on the motifs or pick apart the significance of symbols or colours. Letting your eyes dwell on interesting shapes is thought to allow your unconscious and subconscious to come to helpful conclusions for restoring balance to mind, body and spirit.

294
Music as a sanctuary

Music revs us up or chills us out. In in-vitro tests at Ohio State University, the growth of tumour cells decreased when exposed to "primordial" sounds (it significantly increased when blasted with hard rock!). Fill your space with the former. Look for recordings of birdsong, waves or forest sounds.

Create a home yoga space and dedicate a period each day to your practice.

295
Remove your shoes

As a mark of respect to your intent to practise, remove your shoes and leave them at the door, then light some incense and a candle in your special space. You could also place a vase of fresh flowers beside them.

296
Burn sandalwood

Sandalwood incense is the classic meditation tool, thought to clear psychic barriers to peaceful reflection and deep contemplation and to purify a space for meditation.

297
Meditational scents

The Japanese practice *Koh*, a ritual form of meditation through the lighting of incense, is said to bring ten virtues, including inner peace. Sit, light some incense, and "listen" to the scent, allowing it to form impressions in your mind. Focus on the wisps of smoke, allowing these, too, to bring "messages".

Clutter-clearing

A home cluttered with work files, broken toys, clothes that don't fit and love letters from the past can never be a place of complete relaxation. Such objects stimulate feelings such as guilt, regret and loss that stop you relaxing. Jettisoning physical mess dissolves the emotional untidiness tied to it, transforming your home into a tranquil zone and freeing you to live in the present. An orderly home is a restful one!

298
Winding down

Get into the habit of doing a little tidying last thing at night, once the children are in bed and work is finished for the day. Slowly putting things in order can be gently meditative and act as a wind-down routine before bedtime. Waking up to a messy, disordered house can make you feel hassled and sap the positive energy of a new day.

Reduce stress by keeping clothes in order.

299
Sweeping aside

If you can't get to the floor to sweep or mop for laundry, toys or work files, adopt a basket system. Keep a series of baskets or boxes to match your décor. Sweep the detritus into them, grading like with like: one for work, one for toys, and so on. Stack neatly until you can tidy away.

300
Staying focused

To keep on course, make a list of your clutter-clearing aims. They might be concrete goals – creating order in a living space or space in your wardrobe – or less tangible ones, such as making room in your life for new love. Bring these to mind when sorting items.

301
Be methodical

When you start clearing, begin at one end of a room and work to the other. Don't pass over bags and boxes that evoke difficult feelings. Have someone with you to help you deal with them.

302
Grade your stuff

Have one bag for rubbish, one for charity shop items and a lidded box for precious things to keep. Try to put most stuff in the bags.

303
Adore your clothes

If you love clothes, keep them all as heirlooms (you don't have to wear them). People will run to you for fancy-dress, daughters into vintage will cheer and you'll have a constant supply of patchwork pieces.

304
Freecycle it

Your rubbish could be someone else's treasure, whether a seemingly inconsequential computer lead or a space-hugging piano. Advertise unwanted objects on free websites for collection: try www.uk.freecycle.org or www.swapxchange.org.

305
Create healing ceremonies

To get over old love letters, clothes that don't fit or a bridal gown from a failed marriage, burn the items in a bonfire. Consecrate the event by giving thanks for a memory and ask to be released to live in the present. It can feel good to take a purifying bath afterwards.

306
Detox dusting

A Greenpeace study found chemicals that aggravate asthma and eczema in the housedust of each home tested in Europe. So dusting is destressing; wet dusting is most efficient.

307
Cleansing rinse

Stir 10 drops of essential oil of eucalyptus or tea tree into the water when mopping for their spiritually purifying, germ-busting properties.

308
Wardrobe detox

If you groan every time you open your closet because garments are too small or young for you, or your wardrobe is in such a state of disarray that it is hard to find what you are looking for, try this exercise.

1 Grade your clothes. Throw away ones that make you look fat or frumpy and shoes that rub. Sell online or take to a charity shop. If old garments haven't had another fashion moment, chuck, or store until their time comes.

2 Remove everything and give the space a wet dust. There may still be items to bin. Do it and put away out-of-season items. Then hang each remaining piece on a single hanger, grouping like with like: dresses, skirts, jackets.

309
Eco haven
Detox your home. Discard products with the words "danger", "caution", "flammable" or "combustible" and all aerosols. Invest in eco cleaners.

310
Make a room spray
In a spray bottle, add 5 drops of essential oil to every 10ml of spring water. Spritz rooms after cleaning.
• To purify: cedarwood, eucalyptus, tea tree.
• To soothe: camomile, neroli, petitgrain.
• To uplift: orange, bergamot.
• To relax: lemongrass, lavender.

311
Find storage space
Look for new places to store off-season clothes: try transparent boxes on casters that slide in and out from beneath the bed, or fill suitcases to hide on shelves you can't reach in a wardrobe. Books and work files stack well on shelving fitted, above head height, around the top of a room.

312
New order
After clutter-clearing, the items you keep need an approriate place to live. Set up a filing system for all those pieces of paper that keep a home going: insurance papers, health documents, bank statements.

313
Secular shrines
Group cherished items around your newly cleansed space to remind you of your positive qualities and awaken an inner smile as you pass: photographs with friends, treasured books, scented flowers, mementos from happy holidays. Feel artistic as

Use essential oils to create your own spray to recharge a room's energy.

Find clever storage solutions: try under-the-bed sliding containers or drawers.

you do so, taking care over the position: a home that manifests your creative spirit boosts self-esteem.

314
Top five storage rules
• Store like with like.
• Have a place for everything.
• Put everything in its place.
• Redistribute items from holding baskets at least once a week.
• Pack away unseasonal items, like shorts in winter or coats in summer.

315
Task overload
If worry about decluttering is stressing you because you work all hours, ditch the notion for now. Assess the situation in six months.

Unwinding after work

If work is frantic, make an effort to switch off at home and leave work-related thoughts at the door. Only then will you bring awareness to your home and the people in it. When you are mindful in all you do, whether playing with children or washing dishes, you achieve an inner calmness that effortlessly radiates into your home and relationships.

316
Take off your shoes

Leave work shoes at the front door to shed stress associations. Buy the dinky socks Japanese people wear indoors, keep separate house shoes or ditch footware completely and enjoy the freedom of going barefoot.

317
Switch off your brain

Once home, consciously break off from work by making a focusing affirmation. Use the same words every day for a powerful effect. You might say, "Work stays in the office/shop" or "I work to live, not live to work". Make up another mantra to repeat as you leave the house each morning to fire you up for a productive day, such as "I feel fresh, rested and ready to give my all".

318
Change your style

If you wear formal work clothes, slip into comfortable clothes before cooking or relaxing for the evening.

319
Turn off your phone

One in every six mobile phone users report that their phone causes them stress, found two UK studies from 2006. Users who gave

Kick off your work shoes and enjoy the freeing sensation of going barefoot.

themselves a window when they couldn't take or make calls reported fewer stress-like symptoms and experienced lowered blood pressure when discussing their phone use. Take the plunge and switch off, then watch the positive effect that phone-free hours have on your home life and relationships.

320
Enhancing with scent

Scents travel within seconds to the limbic section of the brain – the part of the brain that is associated with mood and which processes memory and emotion – and bypass the part of the brain that governs logic. Light incense or scented candles after a hard day to help switch off the part of your brain that interacts with the world of work.

321
Yoga corpse pose

This is the ultimate switch-off. Find a quiet, warm space and lie on your back with your legs slightly apart and feet flopping outwards. Place your arms far enough away from your body to free your shoulders, palms facing upwards. Make sure your face is parallel to the floor (if necessary, place a yoga block or flat cushion beneath it). Close your eyes and release all expression from your face. Soften your mouth and feel that the front of your brain is quiet.

Enjoy a wind-down bath with some calming essential oils.

Look deep inside yourself, down towards your heart, then observe your breathing. Take slow, steady inhalations and exhalations. Don't worry if your mind drifts off; simply draw your attention back to your breathing. Try to stay in this position for 10 minutes (set the timer on your phone).

322
Relaxation body scan

As you lie in the corpse pose and, again, when you are lying in bed, take your focus to areas of the body that feel particularly tense. Check each part of the body, including your shoulders, jaw, abdomen and buttocks, fingers and toes. Imagine stiffness easing and tight muscles relaxing as you slowly exhale. Let each area of your body that touches the floor or mattress become heavy and sink or spread into its support.

323
Eye acupressure

If your eyes feel heavy after work, place the pads of your index fingers into the ridge of bone just below your eyebrows, where your brows meet your nose. Apply slight pressure, then release. Move your fingers out slightly along the brow line and repeat the pressure at 5-mm intervals until you reach the dip at your temples. Circle here briefly.

324
Shower meditation

Make time for a shower after work, letting the water drum out any recurring work preoccupations. If work worries pop into your mind thereafter, click them off, as you would a pop-up ad.

325
Purifying bath oil

Cypress oil is calming when you feel angry or irritable (use fresh oil), and juniper oil is supportive when you are going through difficult times. (Avoid if you are pregnant or have kidney disease.)

1 tsp grapeseed oil
4 drops essential oil of cypress
3 drops essential oil of juniper

In a small bowl, mix together the grapeseed and essential oils, then swish the oils into a warm bath before stepping in. As you lie in the bathtub, bring your entire focus to your breathing; take a deep inhalation, then slowly exhale out any lingering negative thoughts.

326
Wash-away sounds

Fill the bathroom with the sound of watery seascapes, such as Debussy's *La Mer*, Mendelssohn's *Fingal's Cave* or Vaughan-Williams' *A Sea Symphony*. Hear the waves come and go and the storms rage far away.

327
Tired eye mask

Make some green tea, then as you lie back and unwind completely in the bathtub, close your eyes and cover each eyelid with a cooled, squeezed green tea bag. Keep this soothing eye mask on for up to 10 minutes to help relax eyes that may feel strained after a day staring at a computer screen, and reduce any puffiness or redness. Once you have finished your bath, dip cotton pads into the cooled green tea and dab these onto your face as a refreshing facial toner.

Listen to inspirational music while you soak: lie back and let the waves of sound wash over you.

328

Honour homecoming

Mark that time of day when everyone returns home after work or study. Make time over a glass of wine or cup of tea to share news.

329

Dance as you cook

As you chop and stir, dance to divas who have passion and history in their voices, such as Nina Simone or Mary J Blige, or samba to Brazil's master songwriters Anton Carlos "Tom" Jobim, Vinicius De Moraes and Baden Powell.

330

Pop a cork

A glass of red wine is a relaxing treat at the end of a hard day. Red wine is packed with antioxidant polyphenols that mop up cell-damaging free radicals caused by stress. As well as reducing high blood pressure, it stimulates the regeneration of brain and nerve cells and tones the digestive system. Have no more than one or two glasses a day and have two or three alcohol-free nights a week.

331

Eating with mindfulness

Keep mealtimes calm, rather than grazing on the run. Eat sitting at a table, clearing away any clutter, and turn off the television and radio before you sit down.

Protect your heart with a glass of antioxidant-rich red wine.

332
Gather together

Encourage family or housemates to share meals: aim to eat together at least once a day, and once a week gather for a more celebratory meal, perhaps with wine, a tablecloth, candles and guests. Notice the calming effect this has on children who won't eat, moody teenagers, and grown-ups too wrapped up in their lives to share conversation.

333
Easy storecupboard supper

All the ingredients for this satisfying pasta meal can be stored readily. Serves two.

slug of olive oil
medium onion, finely chopped
large tin tomatoes, chopped
1 tsp dried oregano
250g spaghetti
30g anchovy fillets, chopped
handful black olives
sea salt and black pepper, to season

Heat the olive oil in a heavy pan, then throw in the onion. Cook at a low heat, stirring, until translucent and soft. Empty in the tomatoes, add the oregano and raise the heat. Allow to bubble until reduced. In the meantime, bring a large pan of salted water to the boil and add the spaghetti. Cook until al dente. Drain, toss in the sauce together with the chopped anchovies and olives, and season to taste.

Nurture relationships with sociable mealtimes around a communal table.

334
Give thanks

Thank all those who contributed to your meal: those who cooked it, helped in its preparation or grew the vegetables. If you said grace as a child, try those words again, or try these table graces: 'I am content with what I have, little it be or much'; 'God has given us all things richly to enjoy. Let us enjoy them.'

335
Taste meditation

Before eating, smell the aromas, appreciate each colour and notice the texture. Place a forkful in your mouth. Put down your knife and fork. What flavours can you discern? How do the tastes and textures change as you chew and swallow? Be as conscious taking every forkful.

336
Watch a funny movie

Sitting down to a funny movie or re-run of a comedy series can reduce stress hormones, promote release of the growth hormone that governs body repair and boost the body's killer cells to stave off infection. Just 30 minutes' viewing is enough to elicit this positive response – even anticipating the fun boosts levels of pain-relieving body chemicals.

Chilling out at home

Decorating with restful colours, decluttering and bringing nature indoors go only some way towards a relaxing home. Happy people make the difference. Studies find that one of the most effective ways to reduce stress and be happy is to engage in expressive activities – the word "recreation", from the Latin *recreatio*, means "restoration to health". To enhance your relaxation at home, try some of the following.

337
The perfect cup of coffee

Relaxed people tend to enjoy short but significant times of private meditation or ceremony. Making a perfect cup of coffee can be one of those calming rituals. Experiment to see which coffee you prefer, and try different coffee machines. Sample your brew black and sweet, with a shot of cold milk, or with sweet, warm froth. Warm a mug before adding the coffee and savour the smell or whooshing sounds. Find a ritual place to sip your drink, away from chores. Do nothing else. Let it sanctify this part of the day.

338
Fridge-magnet poetry

Being able to express our innate creativity makes us more relaxed and fulfilled. Stop to form a line or two of poetry as you pass the fridge; fiddle as you wait for the kettle to boil and set housemates a challenge to complete a couplet a day.

339
Stroke a cat

In a 2005 study, 62 per cent of cat owners reported that their pets relieved their stress. Researchers attribute this to the way in which looking after another sentient being masks our cares, as well as to the act of stroking, which stimulates endorphins. The bond works two ways; many say cats are a source of comfort when they are unhappy. Make a cat part of your family by rescuing one from a shelter.

Honour a moment: take time to make the perfect cup of coffee.

340
Walk the dog

A research study suggests that dog owners are more likely to have a relaxed sense of humour. Being forced on walks each day is a surefire way to rid the body of physical and mental stress. Owning a dog also dumps you in a ready-made community of like-minded people, which has stress-relieving qualities.

341
Downward dog yoga pose

Even if you don't have a dog, try this stretch, inspired by the shape a dog makes. On a non-slip surface, come onto hands and knees – hands shoulder-width and knees hip-width apart. Tuck your toes under and push your bottom up, legs straight. Spread your fingers and press into the floor. Imagine a straight line between your wrists and hips. Relax your neck and breathe. Hold for as long as you can without collapsing.

342
Hit the off switch

Turning off the TV reduces stress. Worrisome news reports are linked to rises in stress hormones, and in a study in *Psychological Science* correlated with nightmares similar to those of people suffering post-traumatic stress syndrome. Turn off one night a week and see how much better you feel, or make an event of viewing, switching off afterwards rather than mindlessly zapping.

343
Take up a hobby

A study at Maastricht University found that men with a hobby were less likely to take sick leave. They had less depression, lower stress levels and more effective immune systems. Look into evening classes: doing something communally with local people you might not usually spend time with boosts wellbeing.

344
Keep chickens

Keeping chickens may be the new knitting: the latest fad to cosset us in the arms of an older, more secure way of life. Even a town garden can support a couple of chickens. Look for well-designed coops and sociable breeds, like the Orpington; if you're concerned about size, choose bantams. Alongside the gentle clucking is the bonus of fresh eggs!

345
Plunge your hands into soil

When you immerse yourself in gardening you enter another time-zone: the larger order of the seasons, the sun and moon and the vagaries of climate. Over months and years, this encourages a calm patience.

Enjoy the benefits of pet ownership.

346
Learn an instrument

A 2005 study in *Medical Science Monitor* found that making music reduced stress. Care workers who did a six-week music course became less moody. More important than results is the camaraderie and expressing emotions non-verbally. Find a teacher of adult beginners and look for sociable group lessons.

347
Music meditation

Use music to unlock emotions. Sit upright and put on a classical or jazz piece. Listen for instruments and themes and follow the rising and dissipating tension. If your attention roams, return to the notes to which sound clusters gravitate, the brush of the fingers on strings and the breaths between phrases.

Joyful weekends

If you work all week, recuperate at weekends. This doesn't mean spending hours in bed: a University of Adelaide study found that a two-hour Sunday lie-in disrupted the bodyclock so much that it increased sleepiness *and* the risk of contracting an infection until Tuesday. Engaging in an activity is a far better way to relax. Try some of these.

348
Keep weekends work-free

To preserve your health, make sure that every weekend is a relaxation zone. Work until late in the week to achieve this if necessary. Without regular two-day breaks, your health and wellbeing suffer and your home support system starts to break down – relationships need nurturing.

Strengthen communal ties by inviting friends over for a lovingly prepared curry.

349
Take a sauna

Exposing the body to searing heat, then a cool shower or plunge relaxes muscles, nourishes tissues, benefits blood pressure and immunity and stimulates a rush of natural opiates.

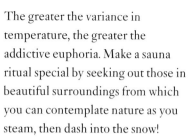

The greater the variance in temperature, the greater the addictive euphoria. Make a sauna ritual special by seeking out those in beautiful surroundings from which you can contemplate nature as you steam, then dash into the snow!

350
Soothing face mask

These ingredients especially suit sensitive skin; use this face mask once a week as you relax in a bath.

3 tsp ground almonds
1 tsp ground coriander
2 tsp natural yogurt

Mix the powders with the yogurt to make a thick paste. Smear over the face and neck. Relax for 15 minutes then wipe away with a warm, wet flannel and splash with cool water.

351
Cook from scratch

Food tastes best home cooked from fresh ingredients. Become a chef at weekends if you lack time in the week: it helps to regard it as a leisure activity. The secret to good fast food is fresh, local ingredients, simply cooked to preserve flavour, texture, colour and nutrients. Lively salads, tomatoes bursting with taste, interesting cheeses, cured meats and freshly baked bread make an easy, delicious meal. Follow with seasonal fruit, such as melon, figs and cherries.

352
Put on a pinny

Wear a retro-print pinny to trick youself into feeling like a calm earth mother. In your new guise toss some vegetables, browned meat or pre-soaked pulses and herbs into a casserole. Cover with stock to cook slowly, scenting the air enticingly.

353
Cook an old-fashioned meal

Ask an older relative about family lunches when shops were closed on Sundays. Give your day up to cooking, using their recipes and inviting loved ones to enjoy it. Then take an afternoon stroll en masse.

354
Create a curry or two

Intricate cooking requires time and concentration. It can be calming to lose yourself in the complexities of making an authentic Indian curry. The ingredients – garlic, ginger, turmeric, chillies and other spices – benefit the heart and brain, helping to arrest cognitive decline and combating depression and stress.

355
Grow calming herbs

Cultivate herbs for bath bags, teas or herbal pillows. Caring for the plants can be as supportive to the nervous

A window box or small patch of garden is all you need to raise a home herb garden.

system as the actual remedies:
- Lemon balm to ease anxiety.
- Lavender and German chamomile to help you to switch off.
- Peppermint to ease stress-related digestive problems.
- German chamomile for nerves, indigestion and upset tummies.

356
Raise tomatoes

Tomatoes are easy to grow and have high levels of lycopene, which can lower high blood pressure. Buy young plug plants to stop "will-they-won't-they" germination stress, and look for bush varieties of cherry tomato that don't need staking. Grow basil too for instant tomato salads (add a twist of black pepper and a drizzle of olive oil).

357
Grow garlic

Buy a bulb of garlic from a garden store and, on the shortest day of the year, plant each clove a handspan apart in a prepared bed or in pots.

358

Make bread

Let the stirring and kneading erase all other thoughts from your mind and release held-in tension.

- 2 tsp dried yeast
- 300ml tepid water
- 460g strong white bread flour
- 2 tsp salt
- extra flour for dusting

1 Mix the yeast and ¼ of the water. In a separate bowl, blend the flour and salt. Make a well and pour in the yeast mix. Slowly add the rest of the water to make a moist dough.

2 Put the dough on a floured board. Knead for 10 minutes with the heels of your hands. Stand tall, breathe deep and feel tight muscles easing as the dough becomes springy.

3 Cover and leave to stand 1½–2 hours until doubled. Punch the dough, then shape it and leave it for 45 minutes to double again.

4 Slash the loaf's top with a knife. Bake in a preheated oven (220°C, 425°F, gas 7), for 45–50 minutes until golden and hollow when tapped.

Retrieve new juicy bulbs when the leaves start to die back next year. Garlic eaters seem to cope better with stress-related fatigue and have greater resistance to infections.

359

Book singing lessons

Singing helps you to breathe deeply, relax your back, shoulder, chest and neck muscles and express yourself. Engaging with music is emotionally cathartic too since it releases anxiety, boosts stress-busting brain chemicals and lowers heart rate and blood pressure. This may account for a study at Sydney University in which singing was shown to help people cope with chronic pain. Find a tutor and free your inner star.

360

Compile your top tunes

Burning a CD of favourite tunes for a friend can be profoundly affecting as you pour your emotions into the job and empathize with your friend. Keep a list of what you put on a CD so you can produce more.

361

Take a nap

The afternoon slump is nature's way to cope with a 16-hour day. Take a 15-minute nap if tiredness strikes at weekends. Any longer and you enter a deeper sleep that is less refreshing.

362

Bump up your exercise

Getting fit only at weekends doesn't have the long-term stress-reducing qualities of regular daily exercise, but every little helps, so plan 45-minute-plus exercise sessions on Saturdays and Sundays to supplement 10-minute weekday walks. This helps to prevent metabolic syndrome, a precursor of heart disease, diabetes and stroke.

363

Be a tourist for a day

Spend a day sightseeing your local town. Sample an open-top bus or boat, visit museums and galleries and take afternoon tea in a smart hotel. Revel in the world outside your regular nine to five.

364

Buy concert tickets

People who attend live music have lower stress, blood pressure and levels of depression, shows a study from Chelsea and Westminster hospital.

365

Go to a comedy club

Laughter lowers levels of dopamine, the chemical linked to raised blood pressure. It also reduces stress hormones and boosts endorphins, bringing about greater wellbeing.

Stress-free shopping

A study for Barclaycard by Exeter University showed that women often shop for stress relief, as a leisure pursuit, but men see shopping as a stressor. A researcher who monitored heart rates, blood pressure and stress hormones in male Christmas shoppers found them to be as high as those of riot police. One-third of Europeans counter such stress by shopping online. Others shun the supermarket for the feel-good factor of farmers' markets, delis and speciality shops.

366

Stop shopping!

Thanks to internet shopping, we no longer have to hit the shops to consume, which makes shopping potentially a 24/7/365 experience. To rest your brain and your purse, aim for at least one shopping-free day each week. Dare to go out without a wallet!

367

"Buy Nothing" Day

November's annual Buy Nothing Day is celebrated in more than 55 countries. On this day, we are urged to switch off from the daily shopping ritual and instead tune in to our life, family and friends. Why not host a swap shop or free concert, set up a credit card cut-up table, or conga against consumerism? Be inspired to look at your relationship with "things".

368

His and hers shopping

If shopping with a man, take hourly breaks: he's likely to feel stressed by shopping after 72 minutes, found Exeter University. Women can keep it up for almost 30 minutes longer!

369

Plan in advance

Take a list to supermarkets to stay focused and avoid the disorientated state that makes you stay longer and impulse buy. Go feeling full, too.

370

Supermarket sweep out

Being herded through supermarket aisles along a route engineered to make you buy removes control, a potent stressor. If it winds you up, keep visits to a minimum. Stock up on a month's worth of bread and

Stay local: sign up to a weekly veg box.

milk (freeze it) and staples such as tins of tomatoes, juice and toilet roll. In between times, visit friendlier local stores and weekly markets to source perishables.

371
Order online
Save a regular shopping list on a supermarket delivery site to cut the time you spend shopping. Just press the reorder button each time. Every so often review your selection.

372
Get offline quickly
Online shopping can be so easy that you're pulled deeper and deeper into cyberspace. Set a cut-off point when browsing, and stick to a list. If you find yourself interrupting your sleep to bid in online auctions, have a sniper service bid for you.

373
Have it delivered
Take the stress out of shopping by having a box of organic fruit and vegetables, meat or fish or a case of wine delivered direct to your door.

374
Choose local
Feel good about shopping by supporting your local economy. A 2001 study found that shopping with a local vegetable box scheme turned every £10 spent into £25 because money stayed in the community (a £10 supermarket spend netted just £14). Living in a strong community buffers you from the negative effects of stress.

375
Trace your food
Being able to trace your food from the farmer's fork to your own fork is reassuring in an age of avian flu and "mad cow" disease. Frequent farmers' markets, farm shops and local butchers and fishmongers, where you can chat with the people who grow and source your food.

376
Nagging food miles
Wean yourself away from food grown on the other side of the world if the thought of the pollution caused by "food miles" makes you feel guilty. Instead, invest in a seasonal cookbook to find out how to make the most of local produce that is ripe, abundant and cheap at different times of year. The *Four Seasons Cookery Book* by Margaret Costa is a classic.

377
Support specialists
Artisan bakeries, speciality cheese shops, independent booksellers and record dealers who specialize in vinyl are a joy. Treasure their unique blend of enthusiasm, knowledgeable staff and oddball stock choices, and take advantage of the personal service you get.

378
Enjoy a day out
By buying from the farm gate, at car-boot sales and bustling towns on market day, you turn shopping into a sociable day trip.

379
Love your butcher
A small local butcher tends to buy from named local farmers and may even be able to tell you which field the stock grazed – how reassuring is that? Use the butcher's expertise on cuts and cooking methods, and have a chat while you're there to embed yourself into your community.

380
Buy Fair Trade
If you feel grubby about the poor living and working conditions of the people who grow your cocoa, bananas, sugar, tea and coffee, switch to Fair Trade brands and breathe a sigh of relief.

381
Safer shopping
To relax about whether other goods you buy contain worrying toxins, visit the World Wildlife Fund's safer shopping site at www.wwf.org.uk/ safershopping, which lists a multitude of products from shopping powder to surfboards to cosmetics that have fewer detrimental health consequences.

382
Shop fair at home
Buying food direct from local suppliers cuts out the middle man and helps give producers a fairer price. Choose local milk in particular, even if it means rejecting organic milk (which might be imported). A fair shopper is a more relaxed shopper.

383
Carry well
Avoid neck and shoulder pain and protect the back by distributing heavy shopping bags equally on both sides of the body (even better, use a rucksack). If you know a shopping trip will stress your frame, favour sneakers or flats over heels.

384
Safe lifting
When bending to lift packages, place your feet shoulder-width apart close to the object. Bend your knees, let your arms hang, then draw the object to your body. Come up to standing by engaging the muscles in your legs not your back. Keep your knees heading over your little toes.

385
Stay within your limit
People who get into debt on a credit card report more health problems than those who don't. If your credit card is stressing you, seek help (see No. 854) or transfer your debts to a 0 per cent card, then cut it up and focus on stress-relieving payments.

386
Save up for something
Save up for luxury items and pay cash. This makes you think about whether you really need them.

Feast your senses on enticingly presented specialist fare.

Size-oo anxiety check

A research project at the Universities of Sussex and West of England found that most women feel "body anxiety" when looking at ultra-thin models. Yet 59 per cent who replied to a study in *New Woman* magazine thought size 0 (a US size corresponding to UK size 4) attractive and 97 per cent felt size 12 women were overweight (the average woman is a size 16). No wonder clothes shopping makes us anxious!

387
Ignore the labels
Don't let your variance in dress size from shop to shop and brand to brand freak you – cut out labels when you get home.

388
Want to look like a child?
US size 00 corresponds to UK size 2 – a clothing size that fits a seven-year-old. If you're older and find yourself aspiring to this size, take a reality check.

389
Ditch celebrity magazines
Confine these magazines to hairdresser and dentist trips. A University of Missouri-Columbia study found that looking at pictures of ultra-thin celebrities makes even women who are the same size as those models feel less confident about their own body image.

390
Empower your mind
Swap mindless celebrity magazines for engrossing novels about well-rounded women.
- *I Know Why the Caged Bird Sings*, Maya Angelou: about growing up to defy the odds.
- *The Woman Warrior*, Maxine Hong Kingston: fantastical, fierce memoirs.
- *Beloved*, Toni Morrison: about a woman haunted by the past.
- *Pride and Prejudice*, Jane Austen: the original Bridget Jones.
- *Jane Eyre*, Charlotte Brontë: *the* passionate Gothic romance.

391
Know what's normal
A project at North Carolina State University discovered that the fashion industry ignores women's changing shapes and still makes clothes to fit a 1950s' hourglass figure. Actually, only 8 per cent of women now have such equal bust and hip measurements and such a narrow waist. Of the rest, 46 per cent are shaped like rectangles (the average waist has grown six inches since the 1950s), 20 per cent of women are spoon- or pear-shaped (bottom-heavy), and 14 per cent are shaped like inverted triangles. It's not your fault clothes don't fit!

392
Make your own
Increasing numbers of women around the world are expressing their creativity and avoiding the stress of clothes shopping by designing and making their own clothes. Join an online sewing community to exchange ideas and patterns, and gain the confidence to make and wear your own creations. Try Wardrobe Refashion at www.nikkishell.typepad.com/wardroberefashion/ or Sew Retro at www.sewretro.blogspot.com/.

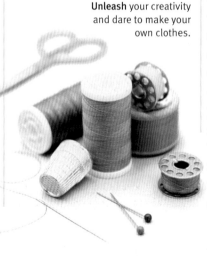
Unleash your creativity and dare to make your own clothes.

393
Wear what suits you
Choose flattering shapes rather than squeeze into a puff-sleeved smock as it's this season's must-have. Buy the new collection's edition of *Vogue* and tear out shapes and colours that suit you. Fix them to a pinboard to inspire your choices.

394
Buy vintage
Opt out of the fashion march: buy vintage. No-one else will be wearing your look, and that can feel good.

395
Customize clothing
As high-street clothing gets cheaper and more desirable, so everyone at the office or school gate is wearing the same item. Customize pieces: change buttons, shear off sleeves, shorten lengths and throw garments into the washing machine with a dye.

396
Flower empowering
Australian Bush Flower Essence Five Corners can work wonders for those with a low opinion of their own physical attractiveness. This essence helps bring about an acceptance of the self and appreciation of your own beauty.

397
Breathe out
Holding your breath can lead to indigestion and create tension in the diaphragm, which shortens the breath, making you look like you are sucking a lemon. Don't do it; you're beautiful as you are. Relax when you breathe out.

Celebrate your body and feel fabulous in clothes that are "made for you".

Soothing sleep

Around one-third of the UK population suffer insomnia, causing irritability, broken concentration, memory loss and anxiety. Insomnia leads to stress, yet stress contributes to interrupted sleep. If you go to bed relaxed, you are more likely to get a good night's sleep. (If there's a physical cause to the insomnia, such as pain, consult your doctor.)

A bedtime cup of camomile tea helps to induce sleepiness.

398
Luxuriate in bed
Make your bed a refuge, where you can retreat to doze, lounge, read or make love. Move desks, work papers and electronic equipment: active energy is not appropriate in tranquil zones. In the Indian art of *vaastu shastra*, the best place for a master bedroom is the south-western part of a site, which is governed by grounding, restful earth energy.

399
Earthy tones
Select earthy reds and dark pinks for bedroom décor. They are thought to be nurturing, suppress the emotions, calm energy and diminish mental fire.

400
Buy a new mattress
If your mattress sags or is more than eight years old it may not support your frame enough to permit a relaxing sleep. Buy a new mattress, and turn it according to the manufacturers' instructions. An organic mattress or one filled with sheep's wool or natural latex will ease worries if you're concerned about oil-based products emitting hazardous chemicals.

401
Total darkness
The brain needs a period of complete darkness over 24 hours and light encourages the release of stimulating cortisol. Wean yourself away from nightlights, close doors, and fit thick, lined curtains or blackout blinds to keep out the glow of city light and morning rays.

402
Keep to a routine
Finding a bedtime and waking time that suits you, then sticking to it, yields consistently good sleep. But you have to follow it at weekends – and after a bad night's sleep.

403
No more, no less
In a study reported in *Psychosomatic Medicine*, people who slept for seven to eight hours slept better and were healthier than those who regularly slept for longer or shorter amounts of time. They also felt better.

404
Check your bedtime
If you lie awake waiting for sleep or wake early, adapt your bedtime or rising times. Use the reclaimed hours to begin meditation practice.

405
Adapt to the seasons
Reassess your need for sleep with the changing seasons. If you can, shift your sleep pattern to accommodate the human need to hibernate in the winter and stay up all hours in the summer.

406

Don't stress about it

It's distressing to not be able to drop off, or to wake early. Feeling tired or wiped out may not come from lack of sleep, but from worry about that sleep loss, says the Sleep Research Centre in Loughborough. Be reassured that most insomniacs gain six hours' sleep on average (enough to stop daytime sleeping); they just don't feel like they do because they are frequent wakers.

407

Don't go to bed

Until you feel sleepy, don't go to bed. And if, once in bed, you feel wakeful, get up again. Do something dull, such as reading a difficult book (avoid horror stories and engrossing reads) or do your accounts. Only go back to bed when you feel tired.

408

Stay up late

Even if you didn't sleep last night, don't go to bed until 10pm to make a good night's sleep more likely.

409

Read someone a story

Have a partner read to you. Revisit childhood classics: Roald Dahl and the Harry Potter novels, *Mary Poppins*, *The Railway Children*, *The Secret Garden*, the *Little House on the Prairie* series or spine chillers by Alan Garner and Susan Hill. If you have 1001 nights, take it in turns...

410

Calm your brain

Before bedtime, engage in a repetitive mental activity, such as a jigsaw puzzle, Sudoku, memorizing foreign verbs or practising some musical scales and arpeggios.

411

Drink camomile tea

Before bed, sip camomile tea, noted for its ability to ease insomnia.

412

Warming milk

A mug of warm milk promotes relaxation before bed. Resist the urge to add cocoa, coffee or tea, which contain stimulating caffeine.

Transform your bedroom into a tranquil haven to retreat to and relax.

413
Don't go to bed hungry

Carbs and vitamin B_6 raise levels of the neurotransmitter serotonin, boosting feelings of calmness. Eat a banana, potato-based snack, lentils or whole grains. But don't overdo it: eating too much too late disrupts sleep.

414
Exercise in the morning

Exercise boosts quality of sleep, but don't do it late at night as this keeps the brain racing. If night-time is the only time for exercise, opt for yoga, qigong or t'ai chi classes, which focus on controlled movements and work to deepen the flow of breath.

415
Take a warm bath

A warm soak relaxes the muscles and sedates the nerves – but avoid very hot baths, which are draining.

416
Skin-softening treatment

After a bath, while skin is still damp, massage in jojoba, argan or avocado oil to soften stressed, dry skin.

417
Relaxing bath oil

An oil bath leaves skin soft (warm, damp skin absorbs oils more easily). A steamy atmosphere also promotes deeper inhalation of soporific oils. (Avoid during pregnancy.)

1 tsp sweet almond oil
6 drops essential oil of lavender
3 drops essential oil of chamomile

Mix the almond and essential oils and pour into a warm bath before stepping in, swishing to disperse. Breathe in the aromas.

Give your skin a nurturing treat with an oil-infused bedtime bath.

Help your mind to switch off before bedtime and increase your chance of a full night's sleep with a relaxing evening soak.

418

Ache-soothing bath salts

Epsom salts relieve muscle tension while these essential oils ease tired muscles and calm the nervous system. (Avoid during pregnancy.)

12 tbsp Epsom salts
3 drops each essential oils of
   lavender, rosemary and geranium

Divide the salts into two bowls. Drop the essential oils into one of the bowls and throw the contents into the bath, swishing to dissolve. Step into the bath and rub handfuls of the remaining salts over your legs, arms, abdomen and back, stroking towards the heart. Sit in the water to rinse off the salt, then relax for 15 minutes. Sip a large glass of water before going to bed.

419

Bathtime candle meditation

Dim the lights and light a nightlight at the foot of the bath. Sink into the water until your eyes are at the level of the flame. Look at it without blinking for 30 seconds, fixing your gaze on the blue centre of the flame or the point at which it disappears. Close your eyes and kindle an image of that flame in your mind. Don't be distracted by the optical illusion of the flame, but build up a picture in

Focus on a flame to
bring calmness of mind.

your mind. When the picture fades, open your eyes and repeat the gaze, trying to hold it for longer this time without blinking. Close your eyes and repeat the mind's eye gazing. Repeat one last time. This builds calmness and inner fortitude.

420

Write down worries

If "must-dos" niggle at you throughout the night, keep a notebook beside your bed. Before you go to sleep, write down everything you need to do the following day. At the back of the book, write down any thoughts in an impromtu mood diary. Then consciously switch away from these thoughts: if it helps, imagine them as ripples on the surface of a body of water. Dive deep down to the untroubled depths.

421
Keep a dream diary

On waking, jot down your thoughts and what you remember of your dreams. They don't have to make sense and you don't have to write in sentences – sense impressions will suffice. Don't try to make interpretations. After a month, read your dream diary back and see if you can spot patterns or link thoughts that shed light on any current anxieties.

422
Herbal help

A combination of hops (*Humulus lupulus*), passionflower (*Passiflora incarnata*) and valerian (*Valeriana officinalis*) can help to calm stressed nerves and act as a mild sedative. These three remedies are often available in combination as herbal capsules or herbal tea; otherwise, you can buy the separate tinctures and then place 10 drops of each in a glass of water to drink each night before bedtime. (Avoid in pregnancy.)

423
Disrupted sleep remedy

If your sleep pattern has been disrupted over a period of time – perhaps you have a new baby who wakes frequently in the night, care for an elderly relative at home or work irregular shifts – you may lose

Writing down dreams may help to illuminate recurring worries.

the ability to sleep properly, despite feeling completely exhausted. The homeopathic remedy Cocculus Indicus 30 can help to get you out of this unhealthy loop and back into the habit of restful sleep.

424
Light sleeper remedy

Sleep talkers, or those who sleep lightly and are disturbed or woken easily by even a slight noise, may benefit from taking the homeopathic remedy Lachesis 30. This remedy is particularly recommended for those who wake feeling unrefreshed, or who regularly experience aches and pains or headaches that seem worse first thing in the morning.

425
Early waking remedy

Waking early with an overactive mind or because of vivid dreams and being unable to return to sleep

can be treated with the homeopathic remedy Sulphur 30. If you tend to get very hot while you are sleeping and/or snore, this remedy can make a big difference.

426
Calming incense

Incense combinations used for centuries to stimulate areas of the brain connected with relaxation include frankincense, myrrh and cedar. Look for combination blends that include all three if your nerves are particularly frayed.

427
Bedtime sounds

Spending 45 minutes at bedtime listening to calming music results in a better night's sleep, researchers in Taiwan have discovered. Choose music that is gentle to the ear, such as Mozart's choral works, pieces from the Baroque era, and works by the modern classical composers Steve Reich and Arvo Pärt.

428
Supported forwards bend

Sitting comfortably cross-legged, face your bed and have a pile of pillows to hand (enough to support the front of your body). Relax forwards, stretching from the hips, and rest your cheek onto your hands. Take a few steady, quiet breaths, then come up slowly, change the cross of your legs and relax forwards again, swapping the resting cheek. If you have a very low bed or a futon, pile up the pillows or cushions to rest on.

429
Evening breathing exercise

If you have a recorder, record the following simple visualization and then listen to it last thing before going to sleep, lying on your back with your eyes closed. 'Relax the skin of your face. Think about releasing tension from your mouth and then try a barely perceptible smile, like a Buddha. Look inside your head, into the darkness, and imagine it as an expanse of night sky. Picture a tiny crescent moon towards the back of your head and watch the tiny stars slowly come out one by one. Feel yourself expand into this space. Then simply observe your breathing; feel the coolness of the air in your nostrils as you inhale and the warmth of your breath from your body as you slowly exhale. Feel comfortable in your body and calm within your mind.'

430
Meditation is much better

Deep sleep is marked by an increased frequency of alpha waves in the brain, which shows that the relaxation response is reversing the body's fight-or-flight reactions. During meditation, alpha-wave activity is higher and, unlike in sleep, synchronized right across the brain. Thus meditation seems even more successful than sleep in releasing accumulated tension from both the mind and body. When you can't sleep, meditate!

431
Bedtime foot massage

As well as being a deeply relaxing massage, this can also help those whose sleep (or whose partner's sleep) is disturbed by restless legs syndrome, when legs become tingly and achy during the night.

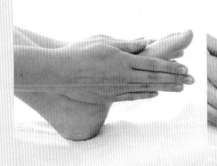

1 Warm some (colourless) sesame oil between the palms. Sandwich one foot between the palms and glide from ankle to toes several times.

2 Run one thumb along the groove at the top of the foot. Massage the toes between thumb and index finger. Circle the digit, press the tip, then pull away.

3 Ripple your knuckles over the sole of your foot, pressing firmly into any areas of tension. Finish with more gliding massage strokes.

3 Enjoy nature

Being in nature makes us relaxed and more positive. Merely contemplating nature sets off the relaxation response – in a study of students who watched films of natural or urban scenes, those who viewed the natural world recovered better from stress. So when we look out on a vast horizon or plunge into a wavy sea, the emotional catharsis is huge. Escaping outdoors forces us to exercise too, a proven way to relax. The natural world also puts us in touch with the building blocks of the universe: air and water, fire and earth. Traditional healthcare systems teach the benefits for body and mind of engaging with these components in the macrocosm (the world) and of visualizing them in the microcosm (the human body).

Get active outdoors

The latest health panacea is vitamin G: a fix of green space and fresh air. Professor Peter Groenewegen of the Netherlands Institute for Health Services Research is assessing its impact on wellbeing, and has found that people who live in green areas feel physically and mentally healthier and less stressed than those who do not, and are better socially integrated. Women especially feel safer.

Adapt to life outdoors and relish the chance to learn new skills.

432
Stay seasonal

Finding out which specialities are available seasonally where you live helps you to live in tune with nature. Track down the first local asparagus and strawberries, seafood and lamb, mushrooms and cheeses.

433
Eat your view

If you live in the countryside, buying local food keeps fields a relaxing shade of green as this keeps farmers in business – it's farmers who look after hedgerows and keep stock in the pastures, grazing lush grass. If farmers don't profit, land can revert to scrub or turn into golf courses.

434
Happy camping

Nature is your home when you camp, and days follow a natural pattern: you wake at dawn as the tent heats up and the dawn chorus starts, and the intense darkness at night makes an early bedtime more likely. Thus, you align your daily rhythms with those of nature. The positive effects of this mirroring – being aware of the synchronicity of our interior life and the vast natural world – account for the success of wilderness camping as a form of therapy for people with emotional health problems. Taking risks when we camp – from rock-climbing to surviving stormy nights – also seems to build restorative self-esteem.

435
Healing nature books

These classic nature books show us how to find inner peace by engaging with the science and mystery of the natural world.
- *Walden*, Henry David Thoreau: a naturalist leaves the city to pursue a life of solitude in the woods.
- *Pilgrim at Tinker Creek*, Annie Dillard: insights into the human condition through studying nature.
- *The Grasmere and Alfoxden Journals*, Dorothy Wordsworth: the minutiae of a simple life in few words, and the making of a garden.
- *Nature Cure*, Richard Mabey: a journey through nature from mental torment to inner peace.
- *Waterlog*, Roger Deakin: celebrates a swimmer's right to roam a country's water holes.

436
Start rambling

As well as reducing blood pressure and lowering the risk of heart disease, walking also boosts the production of calming hormones – just 30 minutes seems to be enough to boost wellbeing for people suffering depression. In studies, outdoor walkers say they enjoy the solitude and valuable thinking time it offers. People who walk in a beautiful natural environment tend to exercise longer, and the uneven terrain challenges the sense of balance and co-ordination.

437
Join a hiking group

Walking is the perfect sociable activity as it doesn't leave you too breathless to talk and you have lots of time to catch up. A group of walkers studied by English Walking Holidays remarked on the speed at which a sense of camaraderie was established, and how quickly those who were anxious because they arrived late relaxed. Walking with others maintains motivation and instils the confidence to tackle more ambitious walks.

438
Conscious walking

As you walk, try not to focus too much on the terrain in front of you. Lift your chin and draw it in slightly. Fix your gaze about eight metres ahead and drop your body weight into your back foot. Let each step be light and exploratory; only transfer your weight when it feels safe.

Take up recreational walking to exercise your heart and keep your mind healthy.

439
Walking breath meditation

Once you have hit your stride, co-ordinate your breathing with your gait; for example, breathe in for four paces and out for four (try to keep your in- and out-breaths equal). If your mind is busy, focus your thoughts on the counting to make your walk a meditation in motion.

440
Wear wool

Wool base layers – vests, long-johns and shirts – are best for outdoors, as wool is nature's best-performing material in wicking away moisture and regulating body temperature. It performs better than man-made fabrics (which can keep sweat in, leaving you chilly once it cools, not to mention smelly). Merino is cosy next to the skin, whether you're mountain-biking, walking or fishing.

441
Comfy shoes for outdoors

Get specialist advice on fit, fabric and linings and on suiting shoes to an activity. Climbing shoes, walking boots and race-walking shoes have varying features to ensure weight descends in a way that aids stride and eases joint and muscle stress. Specialists also advise on whether to use inner and outer socks, insoles or cushioning for shock absorption.

442
Hilltop meditation

When you feel assaulted by difficult thoughts, climb a hill. Sit on the summit looking down on life as it unfolds. Spot people engaged in activities – mowing or struggling with heavy bags – then widen your gaze to the sky, clouds, horizon and tree tops. Imagine your cares are those people carrying out their tasks, and see how small they are in the bigger landscape. Breathe in life-affirming air before you descend.

443
Read the Romantic poets

Walking became a popular pursuit in the 19th century, when urbanites roamed the countryside, climbing, swimming wild and communing with nature. The Romantic poets William Wordsworth, Samuel Taylor Coleridge and John Keats, Walter Scott and John Clare shared their responses to the natural world in poetry. Read them to see how they sublimate the intellect for a more instinctive response to life, and how they view a tree and a poem as an equal emanation of creative force.

Escape the crowds and widen your gaze to take in a broader landscape.

444
Garden therapy

A University of Florida study found that strolling in a botanical garden decreased stress levels; those most stressed saw the greatest reductions. This was attributed to the inspiring vistas, a tranquillity that supports quiet reflection and the restorative effects of wandering in a cultivated natural environment where each turn delights the senses and we can roam without fear of getting lost.

445
Book a riding lesson

Horse-riding boosts self-esteem and releases held-in postural tension. Take a lesson for adult beginners or returnees to learn how to loosen up and let go of stiffness: riding posture trains you to combine softness with stability in the same way as yoga. Not until you relax and establish a connection with the horse will you achieve the rhythmic rise and fall of trotting. For approved teachers and schools, contact the Association of British Riding Schools at www.abrs–info.org or the British Horse Society at www.bhs.org.uk.

446
Pat a horse

Yale University School of Medicine found that just patting a horse lowers blood pressure and stress levels and boosts mental health. Horses are canny and pick up on mental and physical tension. Time spent with them necessarily makes you turn on the relaxation response.

447
Wood and willow

You don't have to be active to relax. Following a slow sport that rolls out over days in beautiful surroundings lulls many a mind. County cricket or test matches are effective – you can keep an eye on proceedings as you read, people-watch or picnic, and for sports fanatics it's a healthy antidote to the adrenalin-loaded intensity of a 90-minute match.

448
Send an e-card

When stuck in an office without a view, send a nature-themed e-card to pop up on someone's screen and give them a relaxation space.

449
Outdoor working

The joy of home working is that your office can be as inspiring as you wish. Aspire to a camper van by a beach or a relaxing hammock.

450
Meditate outdoors

Look for yoga days held outside: in fields, gardens, wooded glades and on the beach. It is especially calming to practise upward-looking poses staring into the sky.

451
Seek silence

A study found that city dwellers may go 73 days with less than five minutes' silence, rural dwellers for 2–3 weeks. In some areas, it's still possible to hear only nature. If you know one of these places, plan a trip or visit an online map such as www.collectingsilence.org where you can share how silence looks and sounds, and contemplate its effects on the human psyche.

452
Seize the day

Make time for nature. When the swell is good, clouds lift and rain holds off, get up before dawn and head for your favourite nurturing site. Call in sick on the way…

Discover the thrill of a pursuit such as climbing and respect the power of nature.

453
Record soundscapes

When work winds you up, browse sites such as www.thesilence.org that map the sounds of areas as diverse as mountains in Boulder, Colorado, and urban streets in Italy.

454
Discover a passion

Reignite a childhood passion, such as skateboarding, or learn a new skill like rock-climbing. Being a bit scared emphasizes nature's power: if we don't respect it, we may get damaged. That's a grounding lesson.

Enjoying the earth

To relax it helps to ground ourselves – to get away from the world of the head, which ties us up in intellectual pursuits and worries – and become more rooted in the present, where we live and our physical needs. There are many ways to do this, from earthing yoga poses to meditation, but literally sticking your hands in the earth is one of the most effective.

Reap the rewards from your own fruit tree.

455
Make mud pies

If you have a garden, send the kids out to make mud pies and join in too. Shovel soil into a bucket, then add water and mix with a stick. When it's sticky but malleable, get in there and do some modelling. As well as pies (decorate with pebble cherries, blossom sugar and leaf fruit), try people (squeeze a lump and mould a head and features). Line up your creations to dry.

456
Compost!

Try making your own compost. If you have an outdoor space, buy a compost bin or nail together three palettes to make a "back and sides" container. Add grass clippings, peelings and prunings (not branches or weeds), plus the contents of old plant pots (if not diseased). Add cardboard if it looks "wet". Get male householders to pee on the pile to accelerate the process (they love it).

You can turn it every few months or leave for longer before using. Reflect on the process of decomposition.

457
Look into allotments

As the stress-relieving properties of allotments become known, so these parcels of land are embraced as a way of returning to nature and relaxing. The health benefits may come from the exercise, the social ties allotment holders build despite diverse backgrounds, the reduced mental fatigue and, of course, the fresh produce: gardeners eat more and a wider variety of vegetables. Beginners may find it easier to share with a friend (the work and the glut of produce). Contact your council's Allotments Officer for information.

458
Raise a fruit tree

Scent, blossom, falling leaves, crops: fruit trees have the lot, encouraging you outdoors to appreciate every season. The best place to buy is a specialist nursery. Look for "heritage" varieties developed over centuries to suit the climate and soil and support local insect and bird life. This helps to root you in your region and to what people there have eaten for centuries.

459
Planting a tree

Try to plant in winter while the tree is dormant. Dig over the plot to get a fine tilth with good drainage; if it is waterlogged, work in organic matter. **Dig a wide hole**, making it deep enough that the root ball sits slightly lower than it did in the pot. Fix a stake and mix in some compost. **Stand the pot** in water for a few hours. Remove and gently tease out roots from the ball with your fingers. **Lower the tree in**. Spread the roots, and trim damaged ones. Add soil in and around the roots; shake the tree to disperse the soil. Fill the hole and add water if needed, then tread on it with a heel. Tie the tree to the stake.

460
Tune in to earth's energy

Dowsing with a rod to find water, objects or minerals is shown in cave paintings and used by armies for mine-clearing. Research at Munich University showed that dowsers had more success finding potable water sources than geohydrologists. To tune in to the earth's energy, take a Y-shaped branch (willow and apple are traditional in the UK, peach in the US) and focus. Hold the forks parallel to the ground and slowly walk, avoiding extraneous thoughts.

If the wood passes an object or water, it may be drawn down, or up as if repelled by magnetic force.

461
Celebrate "Apple Day"

Organize a celebration with tastings of local varieties, traditional dances, songs, apple-bobbing, apple cake competitions and cider. Is there a communal area to plant trees, replacing many of the UK orchards grubbed up since the 1960s? For information on the UK's Apple Day, contact www.commonground.org.uk.

462
Embracing the earth

Lie face down in grass or sand, legs wide, toes pointing in and arms spread. Feel the solidity of the world. Close your eyes and "listen" to the ground.

463
Foraging fun

Enjoy fruits for free, the best way to get in touch with what grows around you. Buy a mushroom guide, book onto a foraging day-school and ask older people what they picked –

464
Mud body mask

Smear this body clay over part of your body, such as the legs, arms or tummy, and then sit back and relax as it dries, drawing impurities from the skin and imparting essential minerals.

- 3 cups Dead Sea mud or bentonite clay
- 800 ml orange-blossom water
- 8 drops essential oil of sandalwood

1 **Place the mud** in a bowl and mix in the water bit by bit to the consistency you prefer, stirring to prevent lumps. Drop in the oil and stir well.

2 **Standing on an old towel** in a well-heated room, smear handfuls of the mud over your body, working from the bottom up in sweeping strokes.

3 **Allow the mud** to dry, which should take around 20 minutes, then wipe most of it away with an old flannel before showering.

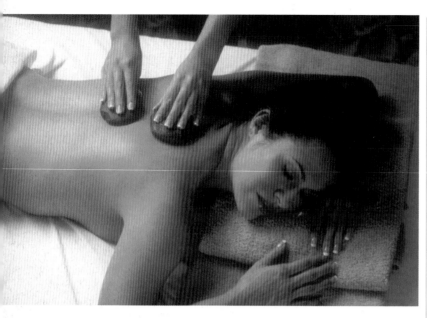

In hot stone therapy, strategically placed stones stimulate chakra energy centres.

damsons, ramsons, blackberries, elderflower blossom, sloes, nuts – and for recipes to preserve any surplus.

465
Sloe gin
This very alcoholic tipple can be drunk at three months, but develops in taste after a year.

large colander ripe sloes
5 tbsp caster sugar
1 litre gin
4 drops almond essence, optional

Wash the sloes, prick each one with a darning needle a few times, then drop into a 1 litre-bottle until it is half full. Add the sugar and gin and the almond essence, if using. Lid and shake. Store in a cool place and invert a few times each day.

466
Visit standing stones
Some therapists think circles or rows of standing stones act as huge acupuncture needles, tweaking the earth's energy. Visit some to absorb the special charge. It may involve trekking over moors or up remote inclines, which is relaxing in itself. If there are customs about passing through holes, circling the stones or casting pebbles, have a go.

467
Pebble hunting
Hunt for unusual stones and take them home to connect you to the earth's energy. Tie a stone with a naturally bored hole to the bed to combat insomnia.

468
Pebble walking
Walk barefoot on pebble beaches or gravel. In China, this is traditionally done before work to bring strength – pebbles stimulate acupoints on the feet. To make a path, fill trays with various-sized gravel and lay bamboo canes and broom handles to walk on.

469
Hot stone therapy
In this therapy, volcanic stones and cool marble are placed on the body; heated stones sweep over tense areas, relaxing muscles and boosting circulation, and cool stones relieve inflammation. Many attribute the relaxation to aligning the body with the healing powers and associations of stones.

470
Crystal earthing
To rebalance energy flow and release blockages caused by stress, lie down with clear quartz over your head and smoky quartz by your feet. Place rose quartz on your chest and simply relax for 10 minutes daily.

471
Relaxing "earthy" people
"Earthy" types are dependable and practical, but if too earthy can be melancholic and fear change. This may be due to an excessive or blocked

base chakra, associated with diseases of "stagnation" (constipation, varicose veins, sluggish digestion) and calcification (arthritis, gall stones, cataracts). Take tissue salts Calc.Phos and Calc.Fluor to counter excessively earthy tendencies.

472
Earthy remedies

If you fear change, try Australian Bush Flower Essences:

- Bauhinia for resistance to change.
- Red Grevillia when stuck in a rut.
- Sunshine Wattle if you resist change as "no good will come of it".

473
Base chakra meditation

Sit cross-legged, spine straight. With eyes shut, take deep breaths and take your attention within, around your perineum. Inhale and imagine this energy centre igniting, like a spark getting brighter. Let the fire become four crimson lotus petals. Fix them in your mind at this point in your body as you meditate for 10 minutes.

474
Elephant power

Black elephants symbolize the base chakra's energy. Keep a figure on a desk or table to remind you of your strength and inner resources. Feel the weight of his feet grounding you and providing security, patience, stability and courage.

475
Earthing breath

Stand tall with feet parallel to each other, hip-width apart. Drop your shoulders, elongate the back of your neck and imagine a kangaroo tail is weighting your sacrum. Feel your breathing begin deep in the earth and draw it up through your feet to your crown. Exhale from the crown of your head through to your feet and back to the earth. Let tension drain away with the out-breath.

Seek out unusual stones and pebbles: ones with naturally bored holes are thought to be magical.

Relaxing in water

Nothing relaxes like listening to a waterfall, watching the sea or sinking into a bath. Studies found that sea-gazing was the most effective way to reduce stress levels. Immersion in warm water is also relaxing: bringing weightlessness, stimulating pain-reducing endorphins and reducing stress hormones. Bathing in natural water puts us literally in nature. Go with the flow like water to stay cool under stress.

476
Watery oasis

The human affinity for water makes the bathroom possibly the most relaxing room in the home. Make it a place of retreat, where you escape the phone and TV, light candles and let the demands of the world float away.

477
Get the temperature right

To induce the relaxation response, bath water must reach the right temperature. Too tepid and it is over-stimulating; too hot, it can lead to faintness. Aim for a heat higher than body temperature – 38–41°C (100–107°F). Don't bathe for more than 15 minutes as this is draining.

478
Unwind with a tea bath

Add an infusion of camomile to a warm bath for relaxing and green tea for skin-restoring antioxidants.

4 bags camomile tea
2 bags green tea
large teapot

Stew the tea bags in a pot with just-boiled water. Run a bath, tip in the infusion and disperse. Squeeze the green tea bags to put over your eyes.

479
Pacifying bath oil

These soothing oils calm the skin and help to lift symptoms of anxiety.

1 tbsp carrot-seed oil
5 drops essential oil of sandalwood
1 drop essential oil of ylang ylang

Pour the carrot-seed oil into a bowl and stir in the essential oils. Pour into the bath just before stepping in, swishing to disperse the oils.

480
Bathe in steam

Steam's heat and humidity relieves muscle tension and aching joints, offers the cardiovascular benefits of a brisk walk, boosts immunity and skin tone and numbs the mind. Have a sauna each week or visit a Turkish bath, or hammam, where you can relax in steamy rooms of different temperatures, enjoy deep-cleansing massages, sip mint tea or switch into meditation mode by contemplating the intricate patterns of the Islamic tiles. (Avoid if pregnant or have heart or blood-pressure problems.)

481
Soothing facial steaming

Calm skin break-outs with this steam-cleansing treatment that also slows and deepens the breath. (Avoid if pregnant or asthmatic.)

Allow your breathing to relax as you enjoy a cleansing steam inhalation.

2 drops essential oil of lavender
1 drop essential oil of neroli
1 large towel

Fill a basin with just-boiled water and drop in the oils. Place your head 25cm from the water and cover your head and the basin with the towel. Stay like this for up to 10 minutes, breathing in through the nose and out through the mouth. Watch your breathing get deeper and longer.

482
Float into serenity

An hour spent in a dark flotation tank is said to replicate the benefits of eight hours' sleep. Dr John C. Lilly, a neurophysiologist, found that making the body weightless freed the brain to stop computing how to move without falling, which he believed accounted for 90 per cent of neural activity. The brain is then in a deeply relaxed state between waking and sleep where it is very receptive. Play a therapeutic tape while you float to steer you from unhealthy ways to cope with stress, such as smoking or over-eating.

483
Swim with ease

The repetition of swimming stills a restless mind and is an effective and relaxing way to tone as up to 90 per cent of your weight is supported and joints are cushioned from jarring movements. If you lack confidence, look for one-to-one lessons for adult beginners or stroke masterclasses. Teachers of the Shaw Method show you how to let go of tension and be more streamlined, which boosts speed and efficiency in the water.

484
Drink plenty of water

The brain is 85 per cent water and when hydrated its cells send messages more efficiently, keeping you calm under pressure. If you work in a heated room, eat processed foods or salty snacks and drink caffeinated drinks or alcohol, lack of water leads to stress as well as tension headaches, lethargy and depression. Drink eight glasses each day, more if you work out or spend time outdoors in the heat.

485
Take a bracing winter dip

Studies suggest that plunging the body into cold water is *profoundly* relaxing. After the initial shock, the metabolic rate drops, which has an overall tranquillizing effect. A cold-water dip also stimulates a release of mood-enhancing endorphins quicker than a workout: its feel-good glow can help to treat depression. It also boosts disease-fighting white blood cells. If you can't face a regular outdoor dip, try it at traditional times of year, such as on Christmas and New Year's Days.

Stay well hydrated throughout the day to keep your mind clear and calm.

486
Try thalassotherapy

French doctors recommend six spa days twice a year to rejuvenate. At thalassotherapy or seawater-cure resorts, you soak in heated seawater pools, are wrapped in seaweed or in marine algae and are massaged with jets of warm salt water. France's most authentic spas are along the Atlantic coast. Look in health stores and beauty departments for thalassotherapy products, and for seaweed treatments at day spas.

487
Visit a spa town

Take a curative swim in the often naturally heated mineral waters of spa towns, used since before the

Roman era to ease ailments of mind and body: try those in Bath, England; Marienbad, Czech Republic; Baden Baden, Germany; Vals, Switzerland, and Blue Lagoon geothermal spa in Iceland.

488

Swim naked

Cool fresh water on bare skin is a sensual delight that intoxicates the brain and is all the more relaxing as it's an act of daring. Try a hidden bathing pool or nudist beach. Or swim in cool water with no wetsuit – they keep you warm but deprive you of an intensely uplifting treat.

489

Mind-numbing water

In Japan, taking a shower beneath a natural waterfall is called *utesayo*, "let it beat water". This meditative practice is used by pilgrims on mountain walking retreats. If you can find a waterfall, all the more relaxing, or replicate the experience at home. Stand beneath the shower for 2–3 minutes with the dial on full power. As water cascades over you, let it clear the mind of thoughts and sensations. If you find yourself following thoughts, notice this then return to the stilling, numbing experience of the beating water.

490

Protect your feet

If you plan to try wild swimming – where there are few amenities – protect your feet with wetsuit boots to make getting in and out easier.

491

Save the ocean

Join a marine conversation charity to relax a bit more when you swim in an ocean, walk coastal paths or eat fish. Look into organizations and decide which would diminish most worries with a monthly donation: Greenpeace (www.greenpeace.org),

Take an invigorating dip and enjoy the sensation of cool water on your skin.

Surfers against Sewage (www.sas.
org.uk) or Marine Conservation
Society (www.mcsuk.org).

492
Surf magic

To feel the immense relaxation that
comes from being at one with water,
book yourself a surf lesson. When
you can get beyond the breakers, lie
on your board and watch the waves
break, the spray shimmering like a
rainbow – then get nailed by the
wave behind – you gain an intense
connection with and respect for the
tides, currents and forces of nature
that puts worries into perspective.

493
Stay safe on the beach

Ease fears about water by heeding
safety rules. Learn what a lifeguard's
flag means and follow it, and don't
take inflatables in the sea. Swim
parallel to the beach, and if you find
yourself drawn out on a current,
shout for help and don't abandon a
board or dinghy. Before surfing or
other water activities, make sure
you're fit, rested and have eaten.
And do what the lifeguards say!

494
Give thanks at a holy well

The long-lived reputation of the
regenerative powers of water are
attested to by the sacred nature of

Learning to surf leads you to experience an intense connection with water.

springs. Visit one that is venerated
with *clouties*, offerings in the form of
ribbons or shreds of cloth from parts
of the body that require healing. Tie
your request for healing to a tree
near the spring as you make your
appeal and cast a silver coin or
votive into the waters.

495
Relax about fish

Oily fish, which keep heart and
brain healthy, can be contaminated
with mercury. Knowing which are
less toxic eases shopper stress. Opt
for smaller fish, such as herring, wild
salmon and sardines, or freshwater
trout and pollack. Avoid swordfish,
shark, king mackerel and tilefish.
Fresh tuna steaks aren't so hot
either: canned chunks are better.

496
Go fishing

Fishing, the most popular recreation
using a natural resource, is a model
of how to cope with stress. Stretches
of contemplation are interrupted by
short periods of adrenalin-fuelled
action, then back to contemplation.
Some say sitting silently by water is
relaxing; others not knowing if you
will succeed, so you focus on the
process rather than results. Some
swear it's standing in water and the
camaraderie and repetitive exercise.

497
Drink solarized water

Fill coloured glass bottles (or clear
ones with flexible plastic coloured
gel from an art shop) with spring

Treat your skin with mineral-rich, soothing seaweed products.

water, then stand them in sunlight. Drink it to imbue you with the sun's energy and the vibrations of the colour: green for compassion and harmony; blue to deepen meditation, creativity and peace, and violet for devotion.

498
Outdoor bathing

Natural bathing reaches its heights in Japan's *rotenburo*: "a bath amid the dew under an open sky". Here you admire mountains, breathe in the scent of pine trees and gaze at blossoming cherry and plum trees in spring or flaming maples in autumn. Or ponder a picture of blossom and mountains as you soak at home.

499
Soothing seaweed

Products made from Dead Sea salt, seaweed, minerals and mud contain marine phytonutrients and ingredients like potassium, bromine and magnesium that calm skin disorders. If you can't make it to the Dead Sea, buy Dead Sea salts or clay in health stores to dissolve in a bath or apply over the skin as instructed.

500
Stroll a coastal path

As you take in a coastline from high up, breathe in the electronegative ions of the sea, said to be charged with beneficial trace elements that revive and destress body and emotions.

501
Calming "watery" people

Excessively watery people have a "phlegmatic" constitution. While flexible, nurturing and sensual, if stressed they can be indecisive or "drippy". An excessive or blocked sacral chakra can make them prone to excess mucus production, weight gain, fluid retention and menstrual or sexual difficulties. Try tissue salts Nat.Mur for watery tendencies, Ferr.Phos for excessive catarrh.

502
Watery remedy

If you are "watery" and spend too much time caring for others but find it hard to assert your own needs, the Australian Bush Flower Essence Alpine Mint Bush (for careaholics) may help you be a bit more selfish!

503
Going with the flow

Water is the element associated with the sacral chakra, the energy centre around the kidney area. Meditating on this chakra equips you with the ability to go with the flow and, like water, to adapt to whatever life throws at you.

Sit with your legs crossed, back straight and palms resting on the legs. Close your eyes and observe your breathing for a few minutes, watching it slow and deepen.

Take your attention to the kidneys. Visualize a stream. Focus on the water: its movement and ability to adapt to its surroundings without losing its integrity, the way it flows around objects that stand in its way.

Make up an affirmation to express these qualities, such as: "I am free to change to suit my circumstances" or "I can go with the flow". Repeat it silently as you focus on your kidney area. Practise for up to 10 minutes.

504
Connecting with water

Meditate on the fact that our bodies are around 70 per cent water. Find a clear space and lie down, imagining yourself as a bag full of clear water. Slowly roll whichever way your body falls. Let everything go, co-ordinating actions with inhalations (to begin active moves) and exhalations (to really let go).

Freeing with fire

Sitting by a fire makes us feel warm, contented and comfortable, lulling us with a sense of safety and cosiness. Evolutionary psychologist Dr George Fieldman suggests that we feel safe by a fire because for millennia it deterred predators and kept us warm and fed. He believes that the flickering of a television set brings the same stress-relieving sensation of security, which is why it lulls us into spending hours slumped on the sofa. Get up and make a fire instead.

Enjoy dazzling displays in dark months.

505

Throw a bonfire party

Mark energy-shifting times of year with a bonfire. The Celtic calendar has Beltane, a fire festival marking the coming of summer and new life on May 1st, and Samhain, the fire festival at Hallowe'en marking the dark half of the year. Hold a bonfire party to celebrate the achievements of that half of the year, and make it reflective, by burning items that symbolize elements of that time you would rather forget (make and burn effigies!). Aligning yourself with the energy of the seasons and changing patterns of light and dark helps those who are stressed by seasonal symptoms of depression and fatigue.

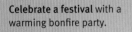

Celebrate a festival with a warming bonfire party.

506

Enjoy fireworks

Embrace all opportunities to enjoy fireworks at dark times of the year – attend displays, stick sparklers into cakes and enjoy tabletop indoor fireworks. Rejoice in man's inventive ability to create light and outward, expansive energy during darkness.

507
Start a fire without matches

Purchase a "firestick" striking flint and gather the following:

dry tinder: birch bark, dry grass, pine cones and needles, wood shavings, paper, pocket fluff, 2–3 cotton pads
kindling sticks: in a range of sizes
logs: ash and apple are good

Make a hearth (see No. 508); put in dry twigs, tinder and a cotton pad. Strike sparks off the flint to the pad. Gently blow so the flame catches.

Make a pyramid of kindling around the fire, using thicker sticks as it grows. **Add small logs**. For cooking, put three logs with their ends together, like spokes. Rejoin them as they burn.

508
Fire safety

See if you need permission and can gather kindling and logs (or bring in fire logs). Fix a site away from tents, buildings, overhanging branches, pine needles, bracken, heather, dry grass or at the foot of an incline (fire ascends). If there's no hearth, clear 1m square down to bare soil. Set soil or rocks around it (don't put stones in a fire in case they explode). Keep a bucket of water or sand and shovel nearby for fires that get out of hand. Watch wind direction and children and never leave the fire unattended.

509
Bake potatoes on a fire

Scrub the potatoes and prick them with a fork. Zap them in a microwave for five minutes or in a low oven for

510
Yoga to fire you up

Virabhdrasana 1 (Warrior Pose 1) fills the belly with fire and helps to generate the calm confidence of a fighter.

1 Stand with your feet together, then take a really big step forwards with your right foot and turn the back foot out a little for balance.

2 Exhale and raise your arms above your head, stretching from the armpits to fingertips. Concentrate on keeping your torso facing forwards.

3 Exhale and bend your right knee to make a right angle. Lift your fingers, look up and hold a few moments. Repeat with the other foot forwards.

an hour. Wrap in foil and put in the embers for 30 minutes. Cut open and fill with butter, salt and pepper.

511
Campfire fun

On camping trips bring a guitar, harmonica, percussion instruments and songsheets. Balance nonsense and action songs with part-singing and rounds and, once children have gone to bed, share ghost stories.

512
Marshmallow melties

Packet of marshmallows
Wooden barbecue skewers
Large packet chocolate biscuits

Skewer a marshmallow and brown on the embers. Sandwich between two of the chocolate biscuits.

513
Masala mix

Add ½ tsp of this mix to your food during cooking; half at the end.

3 tbsp black pepper
½ tbsp cloves
1 cardamom
1 tsp cumin seeds
1in cinnamon stick

Dry fry the above in a heavy pan on a medium heat for a few minutes until the air is perfumed. Once cool, grind finely and store in a lidded jar.

Rub olive oil and ground sea salt over potato skins before baking.

514
Calming "firey" people

Firey, or "choleric", people may be passionate, bad tempered and, once fired up, unstoppable. Depression may follow if others dampen their enthusiasm. They are prone to liver or stomach troubles, inflammation, migraines and hot flushes. To calm, take the tissue salt Nat.Sulph, or Calc.Sulph when immunity is low.

515
Firey remedies

The Australian Bush Flower Essence Mountain Devil is calming for angry people. For loss of enthusiasm, when you feel as if your fire has been put out, take Bach Flower Remedy Gentian or Gorse.

516
Solar-plexus meditation

Meditate on the solar-plexus energy centre to put fire in the belly, boost self-esteem and soothe digestion. **Sit comfortably**, spine straight and eyes shut. Focus on the solar plexus, between the breastbone and navel. Inhale, feeling it fill with energy. **Visualize a blue lotus** flower here with 10 petals, the blue centre like the centre of a flame. Feel the flames empower you with self-confidence.

517
Fire mantra

Before an unnerving event, relax yourself by reciting the mantra associated with the fire element: *ram*, under your breath.

Appreciate the air

Slow breaths in and out reduce the heart rate, lower blood pressure, release upper body tension and help oxygen to nourish the body, while restoring emotional and mental balance. As breathing is in the present, focusing on it connects us with now, easing worries. Airy forces, such as clouds and wind, help us to connect the air we breathe with the life-force: *chi*, or *prana*, that animates all living things.

518
Breathe out toxins

When you are in a beautiful place, breathe in deeply, then puff out stale air from your lungs, pulling your abdominal muscles in as you do so. Then fill your lungs with a long draft of fresh, clean air.

519
Take a deep breath

Lie on your back looking up and exhale. Inhale slowly, filling a third of the lungs, then stop. Fill the next third, feeling the rib cage expand, then stop. Finally, fill all of the lungs, feeling the breath broaden the collar bones and shoulders. Slowly exhale.

520
Birdwatching

Stop to watch birds in your garden, from an office window or when out and about. Imagine flying: swooping, soaring, resting on currents – a free spirit, yet never drifting off course. Serious birdwatching relaxes as it entails being silent and still in places of natural beauty, and giving up control, which can breed patience. Read up on birds. Can you draw lessons from their mating and nest-building patterns and the seasonal cycles of migration and homing?

521
Wake for the dawn chorus

As the days lengthen in spring, sleep with the curtains and windows open occasionally so that you are woken by the dawn chorus of birds as the sun's first rays break through.

522
Listen to birdsong

Tune in to birdsong as a listening meditation. Bathe in the sound, then pick out a call, trying to anticipate its pattern and listen for the return call of mates or sparring partners. Hear a call in the distance, then one very close. You might put words to the repetitive patterns that express a positive affirmation for you – the wood pigeon's solid cooing can be good for this. Or simply thrill to the joyous spontaneity of birdsong that floods out in a seemingly liquid rush of complex, improvised notes.

523
Spaciousness meditation

When you feel hemmed in by cares, contemplate a horizon where water or earth and air meet. Focus softly on this then divert your eyes up into the endless sky and lie on your back to contemplate the spaciousness; let it fill your mind, smothering cares.

524
Cloud-watching

Buy a book on clouds and learn to identify them. This diverting pastime literally lifts you from the world of possessions and people into a place that is ever-there, ever-changing and endlessly interpretable.

525
Hang wind chimes

When you feel in need of a breath of fresh air to blow away your troubles, hang wind chimes. Let the sound remind you of the ever-moving wind and of life blowing forwards.

526
Go fly a kite

Flying a kite is like liberating part of you to exist in the sky, trusting yourself to the wind. Take an MP3 player and fly to rousing music. In Ulster County Community College, kite-flying is used to destress mentally ill students. Visit a kite festival and ask for advice on beginners' equipment.

527
Sacred steam

When taking a sauna, consider its spiritual element. The Finnish word for the steam – *löyly* – means "spirit" or "life-force", and is a way to visualize the life-force: *prana* or *chi*. When the steam hits you, think about what it is that animates nature in its various forms.

528
Prana Mudra

To shed heavy emotions, sit in *Prana Mudra*. Sit cross-legged, the spine straight, hands on your thighs and palms facing up. Join the thumb tips to the tips of the ring and little fingers. Close your eyes and sit quietly for five minutes.

529
Tree-gazing meditation

With roots deep down and branches reaching to the sky, a tree inhabits two realms, offering an image of wholeness and harmony. Sit against a tree and think about the symbol it offers. Maybe a ladder to the heavens, a model of solidity that thrives as it sways, an ability to inhale poison and exhale life-giving oxygen or the regenerative hope of shedding the old and blossoming anew.

530
Vrksasana Tree Pose

Stand near a wall, feet rooted to the ground. Pick up your right foot and put the sole near the groin. If it slips, hook the heel above the knee of your standing leg. Once balanced, raise your hands high, like the branches of a tree. If you feel unsteady, hold the wall with a hand and find a point to fix your gaze on.

531
Winds of change meditation

In autumn, watch a deciduous tree sway in the wind. Imagine the leaves as your cares. Name them and as they drop, see your cares dropping, maybe over days and weeks, leaving the branches to erupt with new buds of hope after a period of withdrawal.

Enjoy the freeing sensation of kite-flying as you play with air currents to create movement.

Lie back under a blanket of frothy blossom.

532
Contemplating blossom

Try the Japanese custom of lying or having a picnic under spring blossom. Feel blessed by falling blossom and look up at the light and shade and the froth of colour. Think about the promise of fruit. Ponder projects – at work, in love – and how they may ripen. You might think about the Buddha's birth as his mother, Queen Maya, held onto branches as divine energy rushed through her and into the world via her child. Look at the five-petalled form of apple blossom, which, like a rose, is associated with the Virgin Mary and redemption.

533
Pin up Turners

Bring the qualities of the air indoors by pinning up postcards of work by J.M.W. Turner (1775–1851), "the painter of light". His sky- and water-scapes at dawn and sunset veiled in mist and vibrant hazy colours have a visionary quality that makes the movement of air tangible.

534
Calming "airy" people

Excessively "airy" people, though creative and imaginative, can be unfocused and dreamy, their heads in the clouds, and can suffer from tremendous anxiety when forced to deal with practical challenges. Airy types may be prone to skin and lung problems, and anxiety-related irritable bowel syndrome. The tissue salt Kali.Phos can help.

535
Airy remedies

If you're airy and lack concentration, or try to do too much at once, try Australian Bush Flower Essences:
- Sundew for a lack of focus.
- Jacaranda for the busy ditherer.
- Red Lily for the spaced out!

536
Chakra meditation

In the Indian chakra system, air is linked to the heart energy centre – think about how the lungs and heart share a space in the body. Connect with this using the loving-kindness meditation in No. 604 or be open to spiritual devotion. Both can ease stress-related ailments and make you feel lighter and more hopeful.

537
Star meditation

This symbol sits in the heart chakra *yantra*; focusing on it boosts heart-chakra energy. The star's upward triangle represents masculine, fixed, rational, outgoing energy. The down triangle symbolizes creative, fluid, intuitive, inward feminine energy. Achieving a symmetry of these two forces is essential to wellbeing.

Savouring the sun

If you work long hours, try to spend a daily 10–15 minutes in the sun at weekends to boost immunity, beat depression and stress-linked skin problems and lower the risk of heart disease and high blood pressure. Sunlight stimulates the production of mood-lifting tryptamine and endorphins.

538
Sunrise meditation

Sunrise is seen as an auspicious and beneficial time of day to meditate. If you find it hard to bat away intrusive thoughts, imagine a down-facing triangle of energy around the navel. See the sun rise red in the bottom point and follow as it rises to the top.

539
Snack on sunflower seeds

Being the source of life of the sunflower, its seeds offer more than antioxidant and heart-protective properties – they have ritual significance. Indigenous Americans used them in dance rites to mark the cycle of the year as a symbol of light, hope, strength and endurance.

540
Meditate on a sunflower

Raise a sunflower from seed or buy one to keep on your desk at harvest time. Use it as a mandala: fix your gaze softly on a central focal point, then rotate your eyes around the seeds and the petals. As you do so, connect with the energy centre in your solar plexus to recharge your internal fire.

541
Salute the sun

This yoga sequence can be performed at whatever speed feels comfortable. The movements are bright, opening and joyful – try to synchronize them with your breath

Grow a sunflower as a symbol of light and hope.

and practise complete sets.

Start with your feet together and arms by your side. Inhaling, bring your arms over your head in an arc.

Exhaling, bend down to touch the floor; try to keep your legs straight.

Inhaling, look forwards, palms flat on the floor, and take a long step back with your right foot. Let your front leg make a right angle (hands on either side of your foot) and try to straighten your back leg.

Exhaling, take your left foot back, level with the right foot, feet hip-width apart. Raise your hips and stretch your body weight to your heels (Downward Dog Pose).

Inhale, lower yourself to the floor, your body as straight as possible, then come up into Cobra Pose by stretching your legs and feet along the floor and arching your chest and shoulders up and back, elbows bent. Make the movement smooth – it shouldn't hurt your lower back.

Now reverse the movements to come out of the sequence: exhaling,

lift yourself back to Downward Dog.

Inhaling, take a long step forwards with your right foot. Keep the front leg in a right angle, the back leg straight and palms to the floor.

Exhale, step forwards with your left foot and take your head to your knees, fingers touching the floor.

Inhaling, come up to stand with your arms reaching over your head.

Exhaling, bring your hands together in a prayer pose in front of your chest. You have completed half of a full cycle. To finish, complete the cycle again, this time stepping back and forth with your left foot.

542
Don't be scared of the sun

Sun can prematurely age skin and increase the risk of skin cancer, but it also boosts immunity and vitamin D, enhances mood, protects bone density and may safeguard against breast and prostate cancers. Relax in the sun for 10 minutes a day.

543
Beat the blues

Bathing in sunlight is particularly calming for people who suffer from Seasonal Affective Disorder (SAD) and are adversely affected by declining daylight hours in winter (symptoms include lack of energy, insomnia, lethargy, a need for more sleep and depression). This may partly derive from lack of melatonin (a neurochemical secreted by the pineal gland in response to sunlight). Aim for 20–30 minutes' daily exposure to sunlight on bright days, keep to regular waking and bedtimes and investigate light boxes that simulate daylight.

544
Homeopathic help

If you overdo it in the sun, take the homeopathic remedy Belladonna 30 for hot throbbing headaches and hot throbbing skin.

Stop to contemplate the sunset and make this a moment of thanks.

545
Sun protection

If you're being active up mountains or in the sea, you can't always avoid the sun. Help your skin to cope by eating deep orange, red and dark-green fruit and vegetables, which contain skin- and eye-protecting beta-carotene, zeaxanthin and lutein. Antioxidant plant nutrient lycopene in tomatoes is thought to protect too. In tests on fair women, it increased the skin's protective powers by up to 30 per cent. Tomato purée is the most effective form.

546
Skin-calming fruit

Pomegranate juice, high in anti-inflammatory ellagic acid and polyphenols, was shown in a 2001 study to extend the SPF of a sunscreen by 20 per cent; it has also been shown to slow inflammation caused by UV rays. Papaya, melon, nectarine, apricots, mango, black grapes and green tea also offer natural protection against UV light.

547
Wear a sun stone

Wear the sun's gemstone, ruby, for vitality, positivity, self-esteem and relaxed relationships. Lie with a ruby over the heart chakra (the centre of your chest) or wear one on a pendant.

548
Turn up the light

Letting in daylight boosts alertness and dynamism and sharpens stress responses, shows research. It also helps you to get over the post lunch dip.

549
Marigold bath

Marigolds are considered flowers of the sun. They calm inflamed skin and relieve muscle spasms as well as speeding wound healing.

7 tbsp dried or 8 tbsp fresh marigolds

If using flowers from your garden, ensure they are free from chemicals, then pick and leave to macerate in warm water in direct sunlight for a few hours. Alternatively, put dried flowers in a teapot, pour over just-boiled water and infuse for 10 minutes. Run a bath and cast in the flower water and blooms, reserving a little of the infusion. Soak cotton wool in the water and use to soothe inflamed skin and breakouts.

550
Sunset thanksgiving

Once the sun has set and the sky is tinged red, give a prayer of thanks. This is a traditional time to think about forgiveness and to ask for protection. Another time to think about eternal light comes when you turn on the first lamp of the evening – offer up some incense as you do this.

Tune in to the moon

Gazing at the moon feels balancing. Its cycle affects nature, from tides to changing electromagnetic fields. This rhythm has an effect on our biological rhythms and the mix of chemicals in the brain. Many women chart the changing moods in the menstrual cycle by the phases of the moon.

551
Watch the moon
Chart the moon's cycle by watching the light or use a moon calendar and observe your own moods. A waxing (growing) moon is a time of energy, a waning moon one of reflection.

552
Walk with the moon
Gather together a group of women who love walking and arrange to go walking at night on the next full moon. Head out to the countryside and walk together in silence to a place where you can see the moon: try moorland, beaches or hills. Sit silently to watch the moon. If you can, make a fire, and share thoughts (and drinks and treats).

553
Third-eye meditation
The pineal gland in the brain is responsible for secreting melatonin that helps to regulate circadian cycles in response to seasonal light changes. This gland is associated with the third-eye chakra, whose mantra is *Om*. Say it silently to yourself as you close your eyes and focus on the centre of the forehead.

554
Wear a moonstone
Moonstones are thought by crystal healers to attune the wearer to nature's cycles, restoring emotional balance and relieving physical stress. This feminine stone is particularly good for women.

555
Nurture intuition
Men and women can try the gem elixir Moonstone for its "feminine" qualities of intuition and receptivity.

556
Sleep under the stars
Sleep with no tent to sink into the blackness of the sky. Try a bivvy bag, worn as a coat, then zipped up, drag a mattress into the garden or find camps with guided star-gazing nights.

557
Eat biodynamic
Biodynamic farms grow crops to the moon's cycle and aim to strengthen the soil and preserve local traditions.

558
Moon nurtured
Look for organic skin products with a Demeter certification mark that guarantees biodynamic farming.

559
Taste the terroir
Biodynamic wine growers claim you taste the life-force of the terroir in the wine: the soil's character and the climate. Hold a tasting to try it out.

560
Grow your own
Buy a biodynamic almanac to find root, fruit, seed and flower times and garden in tune with a lunar month.

561
Homeopathic PMT remedies
• Sepia 30 for irritability, manic (or low) energy, tearfulness, constipation and bloating.
• Cimicifuga 30 when you feel as if you are living in a black cloud.
• Pulsatilla 30 for tearfulness.

562
Herbal PMT help
Take 10 drops of Agnus Castus in water daily in the second half of your cycle to balance hormones.

563
Camomile tea
Sip camomile tea, recommended for calming menstrual cramps, especially just before bed when you need a restorative night's sleep.

564
Easing PMT with yoga
Lie on your back, knees apart and the soles of the feet together. Pull your heels to the buttocks and relax your arms out, palms facing up. For comfort, put cushions under the knees, thighs and head and a blanket over your abdomen. Wear an eye mask to ease tension in your forehead and eyes.

565
Salute the moon
This has a slow, meditative quality. **Stand, feet** slightly apart. Join the palms and slide the hands upwards. **Exhaling**, bend the knees slightly and drop your hands to the floor. **Inhale**, step the right foot back and bend the knee. Move the hips forwards. Join the palms, slide them up and make a crescent shape with the back. **With hands** down, step back and raise the buttocks: the Downward Dog. On hands and knees, push up into Cobra Pose (see No. 541) then scoop back to Downward Dog and rest. **Reverse the sequence**: inhale, step the right foot forwards, drop the back knee, lunge the hips forwards and slide your hands into a crescent shape. **Exhale**, step the left foot forwards and drop into a forward bend. **Inhale** and uncurl until your arms are over your head, palms joined. Exhale and bring the palms in front of the chest. Repeat the sequence, the left foot going back and forth.

Feel a connection with the moon in this focusing yoga pose.

4 Relaxing relationships

Having a supportive family, firm friendships and lots of people to greet as we pass through the streets where we live and work makes us happier, healthier and more relaxed. People with a good support network also live longer, show Californian studies. Perhaps the most important way to avoid social isolation is to look at your relationship with yourself. Only by loving yourself and forgiving yourself your faults can you spread compassion and nurturing vibes. This chapter contains ways to make connections with yourself and others, plus ideas for keeping those bonds strong, from volunteering and exploring a spiritual life to making time for partners and children, and relaxing through times of change, such as pregnancy.

Enjoying company

Though families stress us, research shows that even having contact with people who drive you nuts boosts wellbeing and keeps the brain sharp and better able to deal with bad patches. In a study, high blood pressure sufferers who saw fewest family and friends had the highest readings. Try these ideas to keep your heart healthy physically and emotionally.

Keeping a valued friendship alive can buffer you from the effects of stress.

566
Who's home?
The Department of Psychiatry at Queen Mary's School of Medicine, London, found that men are happier if a partner stays at home or works part-time, as this made it more likely that the family was part of a community with a support network. Could someone be at home for you at times to make life feel less hard?

567
Get motivated
Let the desire to be healthy motivate you to meet others. A study found that women with fewer than six social contacts had an increased risk of high blood pressure, depression, obesity, diabetes and blocked arteries.

568
Think of others...
If you're having problems switching off from work stressors, consider loved ones. Being stressed doesn't just make physical and mental ailments more likely for you – studies show that it places a health burden on those you care for too.

569
Nominate a best friend
Having a best friend reduces stress, cutting the risk of death by a third in one study. Call or text now.

570
Making friends
When we move town, finish education, change jobs or have babies, there's almost inevitably a fall-off of friends. People who stay healthy and relaxed, studies show, tend to build new sets of friends – but women have more success in this than men. In new situations, try out the strategy that makes women more sociable – they "tend and befriend" at stressful times, while men more often retreat into the comfort of sulky isolation and mood-altering substances.

571
New places, new people
If you move to a new town, network furiously. Use all your contacts, from children, work, friends of friends, and go to anything you're invited to, no matter how dull. Wean yourself off old friends visiting each weekend. However lovely, they delay your integration into a new world.

572
Don't try to replace friends
People you grew up with or had babies with aren't easily replaced. Give it time as well as energy.

573
Abandon your MP3 player
Travel without the bubble of isolation that the MP3 brings and talk to new people. Your new best friend or date could be the person brewing your coffee each morning.

574
Dare to do it

Asking new potential friends out can be as scary as asking for a date, especially if they already have a close social network. Do it anyway.

575
Join a club

Scour adult-education brochures and community notice boards for evening classes and groups, from Spanish lessons to knitting circles, and join one or two. If you spend two hours a week in the company of strangers engaged in the same pursuit, you quickly become friends.

576
Try choral singing

Being part of an organized group of strangers magnifies the already considerable relaxant properties of singing out loud. Choral singing involves singing in parts – the focus required to keep to one melody line while others sing to a different tune and timing diverts you from your ego. The magnificence of the harmonious outcome is awesome, as is the camaraderie it brings. After singing, 93 per cent of the members of one choir questioned in a study reported in *The Journal of the Royal Society for the Promotion of Health* felt more positive, 89 per cent were happier, and 79 per cent reported reduced stress (they also felt energized and alert).

Being part of a shared-interest group is a great way to make new friends.

577
Reading matters
Join a book club, if only because it forces you to widen your reading, think about your opinions and get out of the house to chat with others.

578
Become a honeypot
What are you inspired by? Dragons, free jazz, pelargoniums? Set up a club in your town or on the internet to attract like-minded people.

579
Become social secretary
Organize your friends. Try a "Do Something On Wednesdays" session, a mums' night out once a month or organize birthday drinks.

Take the time to write an old-fashioned letter.

580
Connect online
An AOL study found that we now maintain social circles online, using the internet to circulate invitations, share baby and wedding news, reconnect with old friends and meet new ones (giving an email address rather than a phone number). Track the results on your life of setting up a blog, uploading a video you've made on YouTube or setting up a profile on a networking site.

581
Write to a friend
In an internet age, a hand written letter proves you care. Make writing relaxing by turning off the TV, turning on brain-stimulating music (try Mozart or Steve Reich) and using beautiful paper and a pen that enhances your handwriting. Slip newspaper clippings, postcards, tiny gifts and other ephemera in the envelope – the physical items web-based communication excludes.

582
Meet the neighbours
If your home is like a dormitory you leave in the morning for work and return to after socializing at night, you're unlikely to build up local support networks. Take the plunge and introduce yourself to your neighbours. Do it surreptitiously by cleaning front windows, repainting your door or cultivating window boxes. Passers by will stop to chat.

583
Take up a street sport
Find a skill you can practise outside your front door to make people stop and talk. Unicycling and juggling are effective conversation starters!

584
What do neighbours think?
Your neighbours may have similar complaints to you about where you live. Do something about it together. Organize a tree-planting, complain about problem roads or contact the council about vermin or noise or light pollution.

585
Protest to survive
Is there a local campaigning group you can join to protest about issues such as road-building, or playgroup or hospital closures? A "baby bloc" is especially effective. All you need is a banner, some motivated mothers with their babies and toddlers and lots of snacks, books and toys – face paints and balloons are fun, too. Arrive, set up a banner, call the local press and stop the show by playing with the kids and feeding the babies.

586
Guerrilla gardening
Well-tended plants transform unused community spaces. Guerrilla gardeners plant in secrecy, weeding at night and scattering poppy and nasturtium seeds in passing. Get tips from www.guerrillagardening.org. Or set up a gardening group, perhaps with a school or church, and apply for a small grant to transform an area. Play spot the neighbour who's a closet garden designer, architect or town planner and ask them for a little time and expertise.

587
Organize a street party
For local or national holidays or events, if you can't stretch to a street party (with trestle tables, bunting, food and musicians), try an informal street sofa party – ask people to drag sofas into their front gardens or onto the pavement, open some wine and invite all comers. Some communities bring out a piano or karaoke machine for a talent contest; others project films onto the wall of a house.

588
Stop the streets
If traffic stops children playing, organize a critical-mass cycle demonstration. Cycle en masse as slowly as possible, seeing how long you can close down a few streets.

589
Fill a public space
Organize a happening by word of mouth: tell people to turn up at one spot at the same time to take part in a collective activity for two minutes, then equally quickly disperse. A pillow fight is good – those who join in should conceal themselves and pillow until the decreed time.

590
Become a small cog
Feel part of a larger force: find a role where you can act as a small cog in a machine, ensuring things work smoothly. You could be a committee member for a school, deliver leaflets or work a few hours in a charity shop.

591
Keep customs alive
Celebrate local traditions and feast days. Take friends to a traditional dance class, learn songs in the local language or dialect, attend street festivals and buy speciality dishes. Nietzsche wrote that without such traditions, we lose the "healthy and creative natural force" that binds us.

592
Celebrate Burns Night
Around the world, on 25 January people of Scottish heritage celebrate the life of poet Robert Burns (1759–

Scatter some poppy seeds to add colour to a neglected plot.

96), whose aim was to do "whatever mitigates the woes or increases the happiness of others". Hold a Burns Supper. The "bill o fare" must have haggis and Scotch whisky, with readings of Burns' works, including his "Address to a Haggis", speeches celebrating his "immortal memory" and the virtues of the "lassies" (with a repost by the "laddies"). You may be lucky and find a bagpiper to hire to pipe in the haggis and set the scene. A raucous, memorable night is guaranteed. For helpful resources, check out www.robertburns.org.

593
Collective joy
Celebrating outdoors with strangers and, through processions, costumes, drums, singing and dancing, reaching a climactic state of bliss, is something we have done for about 10,000 years. Psychologists say it has profound benefits for our wellbeing and for a community (perhaps by regulating individual and group stress-responses and providing a creative outlet). Abandon yourself with others at outdoor music, yoga or arts festivals.

594
Think on this
The German writer Goethe (1749–1842) described carnival as "a festival that is not really given to the people, but one that the people give themselves" – be inspired by this.

Offer your services for free to give something back to your community.

595
Move in unison
If verbal communication is not your preferred way of mixing socially, try communicating with your body. Moving in a synchronized way with a roomful of other people without having to talk brings a collective joy that's therapeutic. Try line dancing, step fitness classes or t'ai chi.

596
Cheek to cheek
Be brave and embrace a form of dance in which you stand face to face with a partner and hold hands – ballroom, salsa, tango.

597
Do a good turn
Guide and Scout movements bring social cohesion as they encourage members to do good turns. Get into this mindset. You could even volunteer as a Scout or Guide leader.

598
A random act of kindness
Spread goodwill by doing a good deed on a whim: pay for the coffee of the person behind you, leave your book on a bus, hand out lottery tickets, give a stranger flowers…

599
Smile at a stranger
Increase optimism. Smiling at a stranger makes it more likely that that person will smile at someone. Do it on your way to work: meditate on the implications during the day.

600
Volunteering
Studies suggest that volunteers live longer, happier lives. If you don't work, offering your services helps you to maintain relationships and a sense of purpose. You don't have to be front-of-house. Selling raffle tickets or making cups of tea counts.

601
Volunteer a massage
In a study of elderly volunteers, those who massaged a baby regularly during a month felt less anxious and depressed and this improved their self-esteem and social life. Their pulse rate also decreased. Startlingly, giving a massage improved wellbeing more than being given one.

602

Let someone help you

Being part of a community is allowing other people to help you. Accept lifts to work, babysitting offers, looking after the cat if you're away, then reciprocate. Being obliged knits us together.

603

Ditch the humans

Research shows that pets lower stress more effectively than other people! In a study, residential care patients whose pets visited felt less lonely than those visited by people. In another study, people asked to do a stressful task did better when with a pet than a friend or spouse. Why? Maybe because while we confide in them, cuddle them and enjoy their love, they don't judge or answer back!

604

Loving-kindness

This Buddhist meditation helps you to spread *metta*, loving-kindness. **Sit upright,** hands on your knees, palms up, eyes closed. Calmly observe your breath go in and out. **Conjure up** love by thinking of a time when you felt truly happy. Let the sensation fill you. Say "May I feel content". Think about a best friend or loved family member. Conjure up the feeling again and send it to them. **Think about** someone you feel less connected with. Send him or her that compassion. Think of someone you dislike. Try to send the same compassion again. Imagine sending that feeling to all sentient beings, saying, "May everyone be content".

605

"Unsociable" remedies

Sometimes socializing seems like a hassle and we long to be alone to avoid dealing with others' emotions and needs. These Australian Bush Flower Essences help you feel self-assured in social situations:

- Tall Mulla Mulla for the loner who prefers to avoid conflict or even lively discussion, and can agree with almost anything to keep the peace.
- Tall Yellow Top for those who feel others are not quite worthy of their attention, and then feel isolated.

Lose your inhibitions and dance cheek to cheek.

Finding a partner

Being married increases your chances of living a long and happy life, suggests a body of research. In one study, this cut the likelihood of mortality by a third (by reducing blood pressure and the risk of heart disease). In another study, being happily married boosted levels of antibodies so much that it made it less likely that partners would succumb to a bout of flu. Here are some ways to cut the stress involved in finding that elusive life partner.

606

Wear a crystal

Rose quartz is the stone traditionally believed to attract love and romance. It is thought to purify and open the heart chakra and bring healing to those who have been hurt in relationships. Wear a rose quartz pendant over your heart and take the gem elixir made from the stone (6 drops morning and evening) to attract love into your life.

Keep the crystal rose quartz close by to open your heart to new love.

607

Get out of a rut

If you have a regular, happy social life with a familiar community of friends, you might not find many opportunities for dating. Try shaking your social life up a little to inject some potential for romance. Matchmaking experts state that meeting new people means stepping outside your regular social circle.

608

Where do I go?

Apart from bars, it can be tough finding places where mixed groups of people go to hang out, especially as we get older. Drop into social gatherings themed around arts or community festivals and frequent alternative cafés that run workshops as you scour the local listings magazines for further opportunities to talent-scout in your area.

609

Online dating

Once you feel ready for a new relationship, kickstart the process online, which can feel safer and less stressful than getting out there in person. Spending weeks looking around without having to reveal yourself until you feel ready gives you some stress-busting control over a nail-biting process. It's also reassuring being able to check out a potential date's personality and your shared common ground before you meet face to face.

610

Seek a matchmaker

Friends probably have a hunch about who might suit you – and will be keen to stop you falling for the same unsuitable types over and again. Ask them to find and vet prospective dates. Investigate matchmaking web sites where friends write your personality profile, such as www.mysinglefriend.com. In a 2007 study, women were more likely to favour this approach, whereas men preferred to rely on chance social encounters.

611

Modern love letters

Correspond with potential suitors by text to revive the art of exchanging love letters – it forces

Be brave: attend a singles' night to seek your soul mate.

you to be succinct and to explore language as a way of weaving an impression of your personality.

612

Question passion

Our high expectations of romantic love can lead us down some dodgy relationship alleys. Keep an eye out for more old-fashioned qualities in potential suitors, such as companionship, shared values and interests and compatibility. Your best match might not be the one who sweeps you off your feet.

613

Specializing

Look for singles' nights guaranteed to appeal to people with a certain interest – those held in a gallery,

museum or at a wine merchant's perhaps, where you can at least indulge your passion if you don't find anyone to share passion with.

614

Speed dating

The idea may seem sterile, artificial and unromantic, but if you give up your prejudices and cast caution to the wind, it can be good fun. The secret is to enter light-heartedly, and to laugh with everyone else who feels similarly weird.

615

Arrange a date by email

The anonymity and casual nature of an email makes it the perfect way to ask someone on a first date without blushing or stumbling over words.

616

Meet at odd times of day

If you tend to put on rose-tinted glasses after a glass or two of wine and your powers of judgement and appraisal are compromised, suggest meeting a potential date during a work lunch hour or before your evening yoga class.

617

Write your profile

Compiling your profile in as few words as possible can be a good exercise even if you don't book a small ad: list the 10 things that make you who you are, then the 10 qualities that you would consider essential in any potential partner. Filling in the detailed questionnaires of lonely-hearts sites (try www.dating.guardiansoulmates.co.uk) also helps you to think about your personality traits and investigate your motives.

618

Healing a troubled love life

These Australian Bush Flower Essences can help in matters of love:
- Bluebell for opening the heart to sharing with others.
- Boab to stop repeating negative emotional patterns from childhood.
- Flannel Flower for rising above the fear of physical and emotional intimacy with a partner.

A happy partnership

People are happier in relationships, found a 2005 study at Cornell University. After falling in love, levels of calming neurotransmitter serotonin drop and the stress hormone cortisol increases, suggests research. Once these settle, we achieve a more sustaining union. Here's how to work on that.

Unexpected gifts at mundane moments help to keep romance alive.

619
Talk to older people
Volunteer to help out in a care home for the elderly – arts, community history and memory projects can be very stimulating. While you're there, learn something about what qualities both partners need to work on to sustain a marriage over decades. These people are wise!

620
Make each other laugh
Laughter reduces stress hormones, boosts wellbeing and defuses conflict – as long as the jokes aren't humiliating or embarrassing.

Be spontaneous: buy your partner flowers on a whim.

621
Let your partner in
A full working life can barricade a partner and gives a skewed view of priorities. However hard you work, don't forget your relationship. Make time to be together – and be on time. If onerous work commitments last over a month, sit down and discuss how this might change in the future.

622
Be a good friend
As with any relationship, loving partnerships thrive only if you are friends. Take off the blinkers that focus you on your concerns and widen your gaze. Practise listening; ask a partner how he feels, then rephrase his words as you repeat them back to show you understand. Don't interrupt his flow or end a slow thinker's sentences. If you are desperate to interrupt, write that thought down. It can help to formalize matters: set a time when one of you talks for two minutes, then the other one has a go.

623
Prepare to compromise
Relationships are about not getting your own way all of the time. Relax and go with this.

624
Don't sleep on hurt
Try to patch up harsh words before going to bed. A restless night and hurtful looks the next morning tarnish a new day, too.

625
Spontaneous magic
Part of the hormone-scrambling thrill of a new relationship is not being able to predict the other person's behaviour. Try to retain spontaneity and odd-ball behaviour in longer-lasting partnerships, too – go to the beach on a whim during a rainstorm, book a surprise night away in a hotel or bring home flowers for no reason.

Take it in turns to serve
up breakfast in bed.

626

Bear gifts

Look for trifles to ease a partner's
life and make him think of you —
bright post-it notes, a replacement
coffee cup or audio book for the car.

627

Cook for each other

Take it in turns to cook a special
meal once a week. Dine *à deux* at a
table, with the TV off, children in
bed, candles and music. Dress up!

628

Intimacy potions

Try these Australian Bush Flower
Essences to sustain relationships:
- Bush Gardenia for passion anew.
- Wedding Bush for commitment.

629

Be romantic

Champagne, candlelight, starry
skies, flowers and chocolates are
clichéd, but they work.

630

Serve breakfast in bed

Regularly return to bed with coffee,
croissants and the newspapers.

631

Go out with your partner

If you have kids, book a weekly
babysitter. Visit a romantic bistro,
crazy night-club or outdoor theatre
to inject life into a shared day. Talk
briefly about work and children,
then ban these matters. What did
you talk about before you had kids?

632

Kiss and cuddle

Make teenagers vomit by kissing and cuddling. This releases natural opiates and is profoundly relaxing. The Touch Research Institute in Miami found that people who are touched are less aggressive, suffer less anxiety, depression and insomnia, have better immunity and cope better under stress. Stroke as you drift off or massage each other's feet or hands as you watch TV. Let it wipe away cares and remind you of what is important.

633

Watch romantic movies

A study found that watching romantic films strengthens bonds by increasing levels of the relaxation hormone progesterone.

634

Take a break

Indulge passions separately: keeping up activities you enjoy keeps you fulfilled and can re-ignite what it is you used to love about your independent other half. Do your own thing; book trips with friends to walk, climb or watch football while your partner pursues his interests.

635

See a counsellor

If you re-enact behaviour that causes relationships to flounder, try courses such as Foccus (Facilitating Open Couple Communication, Understanding and Study), or contact a counselling organization like Relate (www.relate.org.uk) to work through issues and lay foundations for a positive future.

636

Partner yoga

This is a bonding way to ease out parts of the body that suffer from stress and enjoy the support and warmth of each other's backs. After completing both steps, swap roles.

1 For stiff hips sit back to back. One of you may need to sit on a cushion. Join the soles of your feet and draw your ankles to you. Close your eyes and try to synchronize your breathing.

2 For tense upper bodies, your partner comes into a comfortable Child Pose: kneeling, knees slightly apart and extending forwards with his head on the floor and arms by his sides. Stretch out your legs then lie over your partner's spine, arms folded above your head. Relax, then swap roles.

Relaxing sex

Great loving sex affects hormones, lifting bad moods, stress headaches and insomnia, and relaxing muscles and troubled minds. It also promotes the bonding that can cement a happy partnership. Long working hours, anxiety and negativity lessen desire, show studies, especially for women, making sexual problems a main complaint of unhappy couples. As libido decreases, so does the confidence to give and receive pleasure. Try these tips to revive stress-busting intimacy.

Destress with some bedtime fun.

637
Keep it clean
When you feel stressed, don't reach for a fag or beer. Smoking and drinking more than two measures of alcohol impair men's erections and women's sexual responses.

638
Turn off the TV
Italian researchers found that couples who keep a TV in the bedroom have half the amount of sex of couples who don't – especially in the 50-plus age band.

639
Combating tiredness
If you sink into bed exhausted at the end of the day, you may benefit from making time for intimacy at odd hours when you have more energy – after breakfast maybe, or during the afternoon slump – isn't that why sensible cultures have siestas? If you tend to fall asleep after drinking a glass of wine in the evening, try sex first and wine later.

640
Work less, play more
A large study at the University of Göttingen found that the less sex we have, the more we take our frustrations out by taking on more work. To make things worse, taking on extra commitments cuts the time available for sex. In this study, having sex at least twice a week seemed to be the antidote for stressed workaholics.

641
Anywhere but bed
To reintroduce thrills into a long-term relationship, do it anywhere but in bed – in the car, on top of the kitchen table or sideboard, in front of an open fire or against the garden shed. Be daring…

642
Kitchen aids
Kitchen cupboards are an inspiring place for toys to spice up your love life. Run a pastry brush over the skin, try the light touch of a balloon whisk or the paddle of a wooden spoon, wear a pinny over underwear. Look at what the larder has to offer – cornflour is a sensual alternative to massage oil. If you have a breakfast bar or serving hatch, explore its potential for erotic performances – and don't forget the hostess trolley!

643
Send a sexy text
Remind your partner of your passion when you're not there. Just make sure it's the right number!

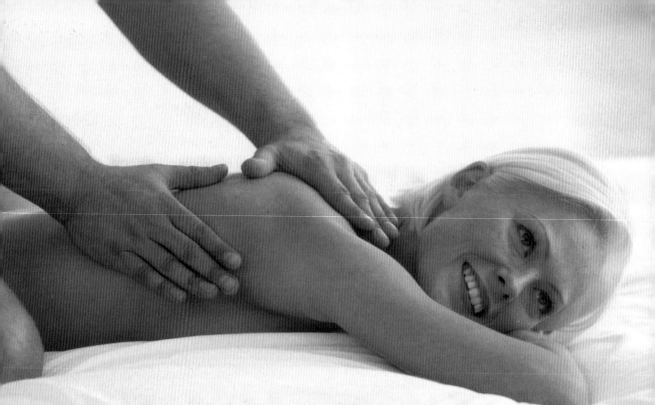

Build feelings of intimacy with touch and massage.

644

Treat it as meditation

If you set aside meditation time, give it over to exploring each other sometimes. Sex is a meditative activity in itself, since tuning into the senses in the here and now wipes out current worries, past concerns and anxiety about the future and embeds you fully in body time.

645

Breath meditation

Lie in the spoons position, with the front of your partner's body cradling your back. Don't move; simply notice each other's breathing. Try to co-ordinate your breathing patterns, taking it in turns to follow each other's in- and out-breaths. Then exchange breaths: as you exhale, your partner breathes in; when he exhales, you breathe in.

646

Feed each other chocolate

Chocolate has phenylethylamine – a mood-enhancing chemical said to trigger the sensation of falling in love – and the "bliss" molecule, anandamide, which may be linked to addiction. What better way to ensure your lover stays attentive?

647

Chocolate-vanilla bath

A box of truffles makes the perfect accompaniment to this bath, which includes anxiety-reducing vanilla and jasmine to boost positivity and self-confidence. The latter also is thought to arouse compassion as well as passion.

2 vanilla pods
12 tbsp powdered milk
2 tbsp cocoa powder
6 drops essential oil of jasmine (omit during pregnancy)

Cast the vanilla pods into the bath as it fills, then mix together the milk and cocoa powder in a bowl, adding enough cold water, little by little and stirring constantly, to make a runny paste. Pour the mixture into the bath, gently whisking with your fingers. After the bath, save and dry the vanilla pods to use again.

648
Sensual massage blend

Make time for a slow massage with these aphrodisiac oils, and see where it leads…

4 tbsp grapeseed oil
3 drops each essential oils of frankincense, jasmine (omit during pregnancy) and patchouli

Pour the grapeseed oil into a dark glass bottle and then drop in the essential oils. Screw on the lid and shake well before use.

649
Cook with spices

Many spices are believed to have aphrodisiac properties and hold long-lived reputations in Indian and European herbal healing for arousing desire. You might like to incorporate the following into romantic meals:
- Cardamom, a well-known tonic for love and romance.
- Cloves for stimulating while easing nervous tension.
- Black peppercorns for virility since they stimulate blood flow.

- Cinnamon for its power to sedate and stimulate simultaneously.
- Coriander to settle nervous tension and lift desire.
- Nutmeg to boost libido.

650
Renew your underwear

Sexy pants for men and women are a turn-on. Wear pure silk against the skin all day to put you in the mood for encounters later.

651
Go burlesque

Catch a naughty burlesque show to pick up some interesting tips to spice up your love life. You could try a reverse striptease (start with your clothes off) or perfect a fan dance or even a nipple-tassel twirling (just bounce up and down).

Cook with spices and inject some "va-voom" into your love life.

652
Sexy room spray

In a plant-spray bottle, add 5 drops of essential oil to every 10ml of spring water and use this to spritz the bedroom whenever it feels less than welcoming:
- To uplift: orange, bergamot.
- To relax: lemongrass, lavender, vanilla.
- As an aphrodisiac: jasmine, patchouli.

653
Sing duets

Choral singing increases levels in the blood of the "love hormone" oxytocin, found a Canterbury Christ Church University study. Practise a duet to put you in the mood for intimacy. Or listen to operatic duets between lovers.

654

Aphrodisiac bath oil

This coats the skin with a sexy sheen and draws on the aphrodisiac powers of oils: jasmine to turn men on (omit in pregnancy), and sandalwood to ease feminine anxiety.

1 tsp sweet almond oil
3 drops each essential oils of
  jasmine, sandalwood and patchouli
dried or fresh rose petals

Swish the mixed oils into a warm bath with the rose petals (strain when emptying). Relax, replaying erotic encounters in your head.

655

Performance anxiety

The homeopathic remedy Lycopodium 30 can help men relax about low libido and just have fun.

656

Remedies to put women in the mood

If you avoid sexual relationships for fear of being emotionally hurt, the homeopathic remedy Nat.Mur 30 may help you to take things a bit less seriously. If you like the idea of sex, but are fed up with being pawed all day long by young children and snarl at your partner the moment he reaches out, take the remedy Sepia 30 after the kids have gone to bed.

657

After emotional trauma

Women who avoid sex because of past abuse could try this mix of Australian Bush Flower Essences:
• Fringed Violet for the aftereffects of trauma.
• Wisteria to bring about a feeling of healthy womanliness.
• Flannel Flower to restore a sense of pleasure in touch and intimacy.

Destress in pregnancy

It's not just important to physical and mental wellbeing to relax in pregnancy, it's a positive health command, as stress has been linked with premature birth, low birthweight and infant behavioural problems. To relax is easier advised than done, however, when each tuna steak or cup of coffee holds private qualms and public disapproval. These tips may help.

The soothing aroma of rosemary can ease overwrought emotions.

658

Give yourself a break

If you feel tired, tearful, nauseous or ravenously hungry, see it as a sign of stress. Stop to nap, snack or have a walk. If you sit a lot at work, stretch your arms and legs each hour to avoid back and neck pain, swollen ankles and carpal tunnel syndrome.

659

Get informed

Assuage health worries by enrolling in active birth or parentcraft classes, and talking to your doctor or midwife. Is there a helpline or drop-in clinic at the maternity ward? Visit where you plan to give birth with your partner or birthing supporter.

660

Nap in the afternoon

In the first and third trimesters, many women need a rest after lunch and after work. Don't feel guilty: you're doing what's best for your baby.

661

Stop working

Many of us work more in pregnancy, rushing to set up or finish projects to keep things going in our absence. By 32 weeks, try to stop work (the organs, spine and joints are under stress). If you work more, an early labour is more likely. Spend time with your partner and children and building social support networks.

662

Let others look after you

In some countries, pregnant women are cosseted by family and friends and urged to take it easy in the belief that this calms the baby. Let others in: shed the bubble of individuality that cocooned you before pregnancy.

663

Restorative rosemary

Place 2 drops of essential oil of rosemary on a handkerchief. At times when you feel overwhelmed by everything, have a sniff – this oil helps to calm emotions and rebalance the nervous system.

664

Using flower essences

Flower essences are perfect as they are safe for the baby and rebalancing for the mother, restoring equilibrium.

665

Do exercise

Exercising triggers the release of endorphins – feel-good hormones, and in pregnancy it makes you more upbeat and energetic, and less prone to insomnia and stress. It also aids the cardiovascular system, helping you to cope with an increased blood volume and weight gain, and easing backache and leg cramps. Women who exercise in pregnancy seem to require less intervention and pain relief in labour and get back in shape quicker afterwards. Check with your doctor first, then try 30 minutes of gentle exercise each day.

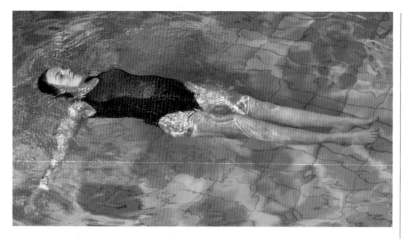

Take the weight off your feet and float effortlessly.

666
Go swimming

Supportive but resistant, relaxing yet energizing, swimming is the perfect exercise in pregnancy, allowing effortless movement. Aim for a 20-minute swim 3–6 times a week. If you can't swim, try an aquanatal class or a water fitness session (tell the instructor you are pregnant). In an American study, women who exercised in water in pregnancy had lower heart- and blood-pressure rates than women who exercised on land and their babies' heart rates were lower too.

667
Moderate your stroke

In pregnancy, it is harder to swim breaststroke with your head raised, which arches the lower back and the neck. Practise long strokes with the head down (wear goggles) and spine long; bend the knees, and keep them wide. Breathe every two strokes. In late pregnancy, when changing arms can unbalance you in backstroke, try breaststroke legs or circle both arms.

668
Floating

The pregnant body is very buoyant: lie with your head back and let go. (Use supporting floats or an aqua woggle, if needed.) Form a star, join the soles of your feet or stretch the arms and legs away, palms touching behind the head. Slowly inhale and fill the lungs, then exhale slowly. This helps you let go, trusting the water and your breath – vital in labour.

669
Do yoga

There is no form of exercise more suited to pregnancy than yoga. There are obvious physical benefits: yoga opens the pelvis, hones posture and balance, teaches deep breathing and strengthens core muscles that support the spine and legs to assist labour. Above all, it helps you to focus within and to connect with your baby, which is reassuring amid all the changes. Ask your midwife about specialist antenatal classes.

670
Baddha Konasana by a wall

Sit on a cushion with the back of the pelvis, shoulders and head against a wall. Join the soles of your feet and relax your knees. If the groin muscles are strained or you have a pubic symphisis, support the knees with cushions. Close your eyes and breathe.

671
Go online

Many women share your fears. Join pregnancy websites for support and stress-easing laughs. Visit the community page on www.babycentre.co.uk.

672
Start making new friends

Pregnancy is a time to cultivate some new friends who can support you through the disorientating "baby" months. Active birth and pregnancy yoga or swimming classes are good places to recruit, as well as antenatal clinics.

673

Indulge guilty pleasures

You can't be good all the time. Many midwives recommend an occasional treat, such as chocolate, to lift your mood. Just don't worry afterwards.

674

Enjoy sartorial freedom

For the first time since adolescence, feel the freedom that comes with escaping the tyranny of the waistband and fashion trends. You are pregnant and meant to be big, and it's beautiful. Flaunt your new cleavage, enjoy the womanliness of your big butt and buy a kaftan (but only if it's in this season!).

675

Stop listening to others

If you feel like public property – stopped in the street to be lectured, stroked or told birth horror stories – try not to get too stressed. It can help to act inane – smile and change the subject vaguely – or walk away like you never heard. Mix more with people you trust who respect you.

676

Calming affirmation

Adapt this quote from Teresa of Avila (1515–82) to help you deal with anxiety; repeat it under your breath as a mantra in times of stress: "Let nothing disturb you; let nothing dismay you; all things pass."

677

Easing aching feet

To counter swollen ankles, elevate your feet when you sit. Cushion your lower back to prevent stress here.

678

Relaxing sitting stretches

These stretches are strengthening and relaxing for the back. Sit on a firm base to ground yourself and ensure that there is no compression in the lower back so that the stretch extends through the length of the spine.

1 Put your hands behind your head. Inhale and stretch to the left, keeping the back straight and your elbows back. Repeat on the other side.

2 Inhale, sit upright and extend your arms to the sides. Exhale and turn your hands upwards in a receiving gesture. Hold for a few moments.

3 Sit in front of the seat and bring the soles of your feet together. Lean back onto the seat, placing cushions under the back for support if needed.

679

Cocooning meditation

Sit with your hands on your bump, eyes closed. Visualize the nurturing fluid surrounding the baby and feel cocooned too in a protective coating. Think about the umbilical cord pulsating with energy and your own life lines – midwife, partner, friends.

680

An island retreat

Imagine a place of your own: maybe a secret garden or beach where you are supported by warm sand. Focus on what you can hear (the birdsong, sea), smell (sun lotion, flowers) and feel (sand, soft grass, gentle breezes).

681

A good kicking

At times of day when your baby is active, take time out to be with him. Close your eyes, put your palms on your bump and enjoy the movement, letting it distract you from cares. Sing a lullaby: your baby can hear from week 20 and may feel calm when you sing the song after birth.

682

Worry-easing remedies

Try these Bach Flower Essences:
- Star of Bethlehem for getting over the shock of conception (though the arrival of a baby is now heralded by a thin blue line not a star in the east).
- Pine, for the guilty feelings many have about not being sure they want a baby, planned pregnancy or not.
- Elm for men and women overcome by the thought of being a parent.
- Cerato to trust your instinct when you feel dependent on others.

683

The urge to nest

When the urge to make it all perfect kicks in, lessen stress on your body with eco materials, and get someone else to do jobs that may release toxic chemicals: stripping paint, sanding floors and knocking out walls. Don't over-buy. All a baby needs is a basket or cot to sleep in, soft clothes and bedding and a relaxed mum.

Use supportive pillows to achieve a comfortable position for sleeping and resting.

684
Pregnancy pillows

If discomfort keeps you awake, try copious pillows. Lie on your left side to boost the flow of blood and nutrients to your baby, then bend your top leg, placing a pillow or two under the knee and thigh to support knee and hip joints. This position also boosts kidney function. Tuck another pillow between your legs to support the lower back. Look out for pregnancy sleep pillows specially designed to support your bump.

685
Deep sleep essentials

Body temperature rises during pregnancy, which can disrupt much-needed sleep. Use cotton sheets and look for wool pillows, which wick away moisture from the head (the sweatiest part of the body when we sleep) more effectively than other fabrics. A pure wool mattress or mattress top helps to regulate body temperature as its naturally coiled fibres distribute warmth evenly as well as absorbing moisture well.

686
Endless waiting

Treats seem more needed in the last few weeks (40 weeks is 10 months). Once you've packed a bag, prepared the nursery, said goodbye to colleagues and scrubbed the house, days can seem long. Savour this time to catch up with friends, devour books, chat on the phone, watch movies, enjoy romantic meals *à deux*, bake and garden. All will be curtailed once the baby arrives.

687
Raspberry leaf tea

In the last eight weeks (no sooner), start drinking raspberry leaf tea to prime your uterus for labour. In an Australian study, those who did had shorter deliveries and less likelihood of a stressful forceps delivery. Start by drinking one cup a day and gradually build up to four cups.

688
Massage your perineum

In the last six weeks of pregnancy, massage the skin between your vagina and anus for five minutes daily to increase elasticity and help it cope with the stress of intense stretching. If you relax when the baby's head crowns, you're less likely to tear. Massage the area with olive oil after a bath, then insert your thumb and index finger 2in (5cm) into your vagina and press to the rectum and side until it feels tingly, like when you stretch your mouth. Hold for 1–2 minutes until the sensation subsides.

689
Pamper days

Spend a day at a spa that offers packages for mothers-to-be. You might get a facial, a back massage on a heated water pad or specially adapted table, a pedicure (heavenly when you can't see or reach your feet) plus a lovely lunch. Enjoy the quiet focus on you.

690
Soft, soothing baby clothes

Newborn skin doesn't thicken until day five and is vulnerable to toxins in new clothes. Prewash baby garments before the birth in an eco washing liquid and dry in the sun.

Wash brand new baby clothes before the birth to remove potentially harmful toxins.

Easing childbirth

Being relaxed can make labour shorter and less painful and the baby is less likely to be distressed. Adrenalin lowers oxytocin (which triggers contractions) and endorphins (which relieve pain) and so can disturb labour. Many say contractions stop or worsen on entering hospital, when the stress response is set off by bright lights, strangers, loss of control and bureaucracy. These tips may help you to relax.

Be prepared with a homeopathic "kit".

691
Well supported

If you feel in safe hands, you are more likely to have a positive experience, and your baby is less likely to suffer complications, show many studies. Get to know your midwife (women who do so seem to have easier labours) and tell your partner how you would like to be supported.

692
A relaxed birth partner

A panicky "dad" during labour isn't relaxing. Many studies show that a female companion is key to a shorter labour and less pain relief. It is reassuring to have a calm friend with you, who has gone through birth herself and is confident speaking to health workers on your behalf. Or look for a doula, a professional supporter of women in labour. Teachers from the National Association of Childbirth (NCT) may recommend someone, or contact www.doula.org.uk.

693
Write a plan

Write down your birth plan before contractions start and talk it over with a midwife in advance. Include where you plan to give birth, who will be there, how mobile you'd like to be, labour and birth positions to try, your thoughts on pain relief and how the baby's heartbeat might be monitored, plus feeding plans after the birth. What would you prefer to avoid: maybe an episiotomy or certain drugs? Though this plan is adaptable and no guarantee, it gives you a comforting sense of control when you can no longer speak.

694
The homeopathic approach

Homeopathic remedies help many labour problems, including slow cervical dilation, nausea, lower back pain and malpresentation of the baby. Most homeopathic pharmacies make Childbirth Remedy Kits, but it's best to visit a professional homeopath who can put together a "kit" of remedies specifically for you, and talk you and your partner through how to use them in labour.

695
Have a home birth

Home births can be less stressful as you can eat, drink and pee when you want, use the rooms that you want and arrange lighting, heating and sounds for maximum comfort. You can be mobile, aren't tied to a monitor and retain more control over the speed of labour (without being rushed to suit hospital routine), all of which make intervention less likely. Most relaxing is that often more than one midwife attends you (in hospital most women share midwives and endure changes of staff as shifts change). Research suggests home birth is at least as safe as a hospital birth, and likely to lead to less intervention and speedier physical and mental recovery.

696

Control your surroundings

Surround yourself with relaxing items: candles, a soft blanket, your favourite pillows, a birthing ball, photographs of older children, the baby's first toy. Ask for dim lights and put on music that makes you zone out, whether it's Bulgarian folk singing, Northern soul, long jazz tunes or modern minimalist pieces.

697

Ask for information

Put in the birth plan that you want to be informed throughout and told you're doing well. If medical matters scare you, your body will tense and halt the hormone that drives labour.

698

Stay upright

Remain upright as gravity makes contractions more effective and aids the baby's journey through the birth canal. Squatting increases the size of the pelvic outlet, maybe making the second stage less stressful. Why tax your body and baby by lying down?

699

Keep moving

Women who are mobile in the labour room tend to have shorter labours and fewer drugs than those who recline on a bed. Pace around, get onto all fours, circle your hips like a belly dancer, place your arms against a wall and pad your feet up and down – the positions your body tells you to get into tend to support efficient labouring.

700

Get in the bath

In the early stages of labour, warm water relieves pain. A birthing pool is best because it has space to move around and firm sides to rest forwards onto. Research links use of birthing pools with fewer epidurals and pethidine, suggesting this helps to manage pain, and reduces the chance of tearing or an episiotomy. If you want to use one at hospital, ask beforehand about how likely it is to be available and how many have managed to use it in recent months. Hire a pool for home births.

701

Visualization focus

It may help to visualize yourself as a surfer, riding the waves of contractions – always on top of them and coming into shore. Other women find a lotus flower or rose a useful point of focus. Imagine the flower first as a tightly closed bud. With each contraction, sense its petals gently opening and becoming more beautiful.

702

Relish the breaks

Between contractions there is no pain. Keep this as a mantra. In a break, sip water and relax the shoulders and chest, toes and jaw. Do you want to change the music or

Focus on a rose: its blossoming petals a metaphor for the steady progression of your labour.

Relaxed, steady breathing can help to release tension in you and, in turn, your baby.

tension on the out-breath, especially around the shoulders and chest, an antidote to the stress response. Try the exercise *so-ham*: say *so* silently as you inhale and sigh out *ham* through soft, open lips. *So* refers to you, *ham* to everything in existence, including those helping you and your baby.

706
Breath support
Teach your birth partner the *so-ham* technique; if you panic and breathe shallowly he can remind you of the pain-relieving out-breath. If you're beyond words, have your partner blow on your face to call you back to the calming out-breath.

707
Relax your throat
Sighing relaxes the throat, which helps to release the pelvic floor. Try voicing out-breaths. This lengthens exhalations, which calms the body, making pain more bearable. Let each in-breath be quiet and natural.

708
Snacking
Eat a little to cope with a long labour. A Canadian study suggests that women who can eat at will don't have worse outcomes. In early labour try a calming carb snack, such as a wholemeal sandwich, a banana or oatcakes, but don't overeat.

lights? Joke with midwives and rest to store the energy to engage with the action and ride the contractions.

703
No clocks
Remove clocks and watches from the room. It's not relaxing to know that your labour is going on for ever.

704
Hypnobirth
Investigate this therapy where you and your birthing partner induce a deep state of relaxation through self-hypnosis, breathing techniques and ways of welcoming the "surge" (contraction). It correlates in British, Chinese and American studies with shorter labour, less pain medication, fewer complications and a calmer mother. At HypnoBirthing® classes you sever connections between the concepts of birth, fear and pain and learn ways to keep the birthing room calm. This method is also said to have a natural epidural effect.

705
The power of the breath
Deep, rhythmical breaths maximize the oxygen available to you and your baby on the in-breath and release

709
Supportive massage

Massage can be a non-verbal support, stimulating the release of endorphins. A study found that this helped women manage pain better, have shorter labours, relax and be less likely to suffer postnatal depression.

710
Get your hands off

If you find being touched in labour annoying, just ask someone to stop. Too tentative a touch in the wrong place or too fast can make you tense.

711
Shoulder massage

Ask a partner to rest his forearms on your shoulders, then to rotate the thumb tips in the bony shoulder girdle and around shoulder blades. He could follow with long alternate palm strokes down either side of the spine, one hand always on the body.

712
Lower back massage

There are pain-release points on the bony ridge of the sacrum. Get your partner to apply pressure with his thumbs, starting at the centre of the sitting bones and moving out.

A quick, healthy snack in early labour fuels you to endure the hours ahead.

713
Leg massage

Stand with the forearms on a wall, one foot back. Lean into the wall and ask your partner to stroke your calves.

714
Wear woolly socks

In labour feet can get chilled, which causes tension elsewhere. Wear pure new wool socks or felted slippers.

715
Rescue me!

Put a few drops of Bach Flowers Rescue Remedy in a glass of water with a bendy straw so it's accessible whatever position you are in. Sip between contractions and if you feel overwhelmed, shocked, afraid or beyond your limit to bring calmness and belief that you can cope.

716
Facial spritzer

Keep a water spritzer in the fridge or a cool pack and have someone spray your face when the birthing pool feels too warm or you are exhausted by the effort of pushing.

717
Lip balm

Breathing through your mouth for hours can result in chapped, sore lips. Use a lip salve blended from natural waxes (shea butter, jojoba, beeswax) to avoid body-stressing petrochemicals.

Relax with a new baby

Being alone with a new baby can be as terrifying as it is joyous, especially if you have no experience of babies until you have them in your 30s, and have no family close by to give practical support. Colicky crying, sleepless nights, sore nipples and stitches are no recipe for relaxation, but here are some ways to ease into this strange, new, wonderful life.

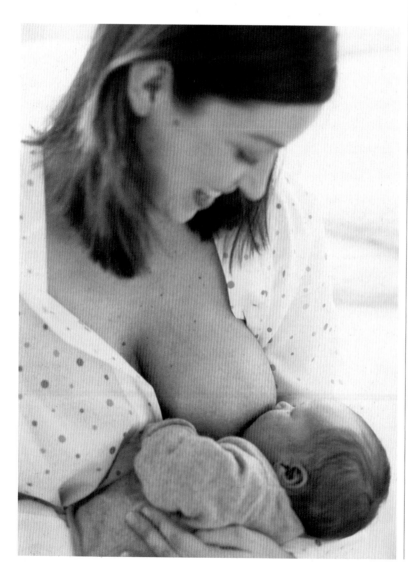

718

Stay in bed

When you and your baby get home, ask for fresh sheets, clean nightwear, pile up pillows and take to your bed together. See visitors here – if you're up and about, you may find yourself making tea, baking cakes, opening champagne, arranging flowers and even acting as taxi driver. When you can't see what's going on, you're less likely to care about chaos and mess.

719

Make time and space

Above all, you need space to lie and look at your baby, tuning into each other and taking advantage of the intense eye-contact newborn babies give. Cut through the stress to enjoy a "babymoon" period. It will seem incredibly distant after a few weeks.

720

40-day retreat

Many cultures have a "lying-in" time, when a woman is cared for by family and friends for 40 days. She is massaged, fed healthy food to build her up and help milk production and the baby is whisked away so she can rest. Modern life expects us to be back to the supermarket within days. Let others cook for at least a week.

Getting comfortable before settling for a feed helps your baby to latch on.

721
Refuse visitors
Many people visit on day three when milk comes in, the baby is wakeful, your euphoria is being eroded by lack of sleep and hormones go crazy. Have someone bat them away.

722
Ask for gifts
Everyone brings baby presents. Ask your partner or mother to hint to visitors that they could bring you something – an effective eye cream, expensive moisturizer, new clothes or jewellery or a massage therapist who specializes in maternity care.

723
Perineum destressing
Witch-hazel or arnica calm swelling and soreness around the perineum, or put a few drops of Marigold tincture (*calendula officinalis*) in a bath and on your sanitary towel for its healing and antiseptic properties.

724
Post-natal homeopathy
Try some destressing remedies:
- Arnica 30 and Hypericum 30: take alternately each hour after a Caesarean to speed healing and ease pain.
- Aconite 30 for shock, following a hard delivery and to bring you back to reality if you feel "out-of-it".

Seek natural remedies: a cool cabbage leaf can soothe inflamed breasts.

- Chamomilla 30 eases after-pains.
- Phytolacca 30 for breast soreness, or for engorged breasts before the baby learns to feed efficiently.

725
Comfy feeding
Get comfortable to ensure a good flow of milk, correct latching-on and a happy baby. Sit with both feet on the floor, your legs supported. Support the lower back with cushions or a blanket, and support your arms at a right angle. Keep warm with a blanket and have a drink to hand and diversions for long feeds. Don't worry; soon you'll be feeding in a sling as you cook dinner, browse the shops or go on a protest march.

726
Relaxing to feed
If you and your baby get stressed, try this meditative technique that helps you to ignore distractions.
Imagine drawing breath from the earth up through the spine. As you exhale, see a fountain of white light flowing out of your head, protecting you and your baby in a bubble.
After a few breaths, combine with Bumblebee Breathing (see No. 26). Your baby will then associate your gentle breathing with relaxed feeds.

727
Green relief
Place a fresh Savoy cabbage leaf around each breast inside your bra to soothe hot, inflamed breasts. First beat the leaves a bit to soften them and release the cooling juice.

728
Sucky babies
Breastfeeding benefits you both, but be aware that breastfed babies spend less time quietly sleeping than formula-fed ones. It's not your fault!

729
Tea for milk
Take nettle tea to up milk supply, or the homeopathic remedy Urtica Urens 30 twice daily for a week.

730
Milky bath
To increase milk flow, bathe (without baby) with 10 drops of essential oil of geranium or 6 drops of essential oil of fennel (not if you have allergies).

731
Organic nursing pads

Opt for non-scratchy, ultra-absorbent hemp, Danish untreated merino wool (natural lanolin is antibacterial) or untreated silk and wool mixes.

732
Call a helpline

If feeding is stressful for you and your baby, get advice. Try the National Childbirth Trust (NCT) helpline or, if there is a hospital feeding counsellor, insist they visit, or ask an NCT or La Leche League counsellor – www. laleche.org.uk – for local support.

733
Coping at night

If your baby is awake all night, bring him to bed. Use a night-light to help with latching on and keep a drink and warm wrap to hand. Don't change him unless you need to and keep changing equipment close by.

734
Swaddling

Young babies find it comforting to have jerky legs and arms secured. Lie your baby on a cotton cot sheet, the long side horizontal. Wrap one end, then the other, across his body.

Some babies find being gently, but securely, swaddled intensely calming.

735
Warm the cot

When you remove your baby from his cot for a night-time feed, pop a warm (not hot) water bottle in his place so it's warm when you put him back in. (Don't forget to take it out.)

736
Learn to feed lying down

Second-time mothers swear by this technique, which allows you to doze through night-time feeds. Lie on your side and pull your baby towards your lower breast. Watch that the bed covers are well away from his face (you may need a shawl for your shoulders). For safety, put the baby back in his cot when you have finished feeding.

737
Feed in the bath

As a last resort, get into a warm bath with a distressed baby. As the water calms both of you, establish feeding here. Be sure that your baby's head is well supported out of the water and don't drop off!

738
Natural lambskins

A University of Cambridge study found that babies who are put down on a lambskin cry less, settle quicker after feeds and lie quietly for longer.

Many European mothers swear by them to keep babies happy at night, too, but midwives worry about overheating. Choose undyed, unbleached skins designed for babies (or organically tanned skins using tannin from a mimosa tree). Easy to carry, they make any new place cosily familiar.

739
Buy a new outfit
Sick of pregnancy clothes and can't fit into skinny jeans? Buy an outfit online (try www.topshop.com).

740
Embracing change
Becoming a mother is life-changing. If you don't take to it immediately, try Australian Bush Flower Essence Bottlebrush to help you adapt to this change that challenges your identity.

741
Wise words
"Cling not to that which changes" urged the Buddha. Relate this to your new life and its inevitable losses – of being a couple, of friendships with non-baby people, of lack of responsibilities and of being on your own. Forgive yourself for wanting things as they were.

742
Perfection is impossible!
Motherhood is an undervalued (and unpaid) full-time job, and no mother ever feels she is getting it right. Now is not the time to become a perfectionist. To get through each day, allow yourself to get things wrong, and learn to ask for help when you need it.

743
Soothing strokes
Stroking and touching is a great way to get to know your new baby. It gives you confidence in handling those fragile limbs, and is a practical way to demonstrate your love if you feel numb after the birth.

1 With your hand gently resting on your baby's head, use the tip of your thumb to make light, soothing strokes from her forehead out to her temple. Talk to your baby while you do this and make eye contact if she is awake.

2 Use your fingertips in a circular stroking action to gently massage down from your baby's thighs to her knees, then work down from her knees to the ankles. Repeat these relaxing circular strokes on the other leg.

Enjoying the first year

Scandinavian studies show that a child's sleep patterns are a predictor of your stress. Sleep deprivation elevates stress in babies too and, as they get older, can resemble ADHD (Attention Deficit Hyperactivity Disorder). We have the power to teach our children how to relax and sleep better. Here are some tips for consistent sleep and relaxed play.

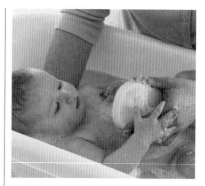

An evening bath can become a reassuring bedtime ritual for your baby.

744
A relaxed bedtime
Teaching a child how to go to sleep is not easy, but is one of the most empowering and relaxing skills you can pass on as a parent. A consistent bedtime routine is the way. Feel brave enough to begin it tonight.

745
Setting a time
If you wait until your baby is sleepy before putting her to bed, you might be up all night. Some babies always seem alert and bright-eyed, but overwrought activity can be a sign of tiredness – it also makes it harder for a child to settle and leads to more night waking. Start by setting a consistent bedtime, making it early enough to equip your infant with the resources to cope with a day's happy exploring and learning, and to give you time to relax. However hard it may seem, do stick to this time. Eventually, your child will become sleepy on cue.

746
Calming bedtime routine
Babies relax when they know what comes next, and this helps them to drift to sleep. A routine might include a meal, play, bathtime, milk, pyjamas and teeth-brushing, a story, cuddles and a song. Tuck her in, kiss her goodnight and leave while she's dozy but awake. If she gets agitated, go back to comfort her, then leave, increasing the amount of time you spend outside each time she fusses (this lets her discover how to settle herself, rather than relying on you). The trick is repetition; a bedtime routine only becomes reassuring if you repeat it every night at the same time. If this means disrupting your adult life for a while, go with it.

747
Soothing sounds
Being soothed to sleep by familiar music is so effective that it's used in hospitals and babycare centres across North America. Research with premature babies shows that music at bedtime not only calms a baby and reduces pain, it boosts oxygen levels, weight gain, sucking ability and head circumference (a sign of intelligence).

748
Tried and tested baby music
As you settle your baby in his cot, put on a CD of calming classical music especially chosen to appeal to infants, or select womb or nature sounds. Make sure the tracks last at least 15 minutes. These pieces are recommended:
• *Six Marimbas*, Steve Reich: 16 minutes of gradually evolving soundscape.
• *Descending Moonshine Dervishes*, Terry Riley: rippling waves of sound.
• *Soothing Sounds for Baby*, Raymond Scott: sonic experimentation that sounds odd to adults, but babies love this music.

749

Sedating darkness

Fit blackout blinds at nursery windows to keep out chinks of light that stimulate your baby to wake early in the morning and try to wean your baby away from nightlights. Complete darkness seems to help a child to adapt to a regular sleep cycle. A report in *Nature* has also linked sleeping with a nightlight under the age of two with myopia (short-sightedness).

750

Time for a nap

Napping during the day seems to help your baby's night-time sleep pattern – and it gets *you* through the rest of the day, too. If possible, rig up a hammock somewhere shady and get in with your baby, letting the swinging action lead you both to the land of dreams.

751

Easing colic

If abdominal spasms prevent your baby from relaxing during the evening, try yoga's wind-relieving pose. Lie your baby on his back and gently grasp his ankles. Press his knees towards his chest for a couple of seconds, then slowly straighten his legs. Repeat this exercise a few times. If your baby enjoys it, try cycling alternate legs.

752

Secure holds

Use these ideas in the evening to pacify a colicky or restless infant.
Hold your baby horizontally, facing out, his back against your abdomen. Wrap an arm under and around his chest, with his head on your forearm. Put your other hand between his legs to rest softly on his tummy. Walk around to show him the world.
Roll your baby to face the floor, with one arm and hand around his chest, the other on his tummy. Swing gently from side to side.

753

Camomile for testy babies

Look for homeopathic Chamomilla granules to soothe colicky pains, teething, tummy upsets and fractious crying.

754

Easing warmth

Half fill a hot-water bottle with lukewarm water, then wrap it in a soft cover and hold gently against your baby's abdomen to relieve colicky spasms.

Close contact and soothing sounds help to relax your baby before bedtime.

755
Bathe together

Baby baths can feel safer for a newborn baby, but they can also be restricting and hard for a baby and stressful for your upper back and shoulders. Don't be afraid to see if your baby prefers bathing with you, skin to skin. You won't be able to enjoy really hot water, but you do get to play games with your baby and watch her relaxing and opening her limbs. Make sure her head is well supported, and finish the bath before she looks tired.

756
Language bath

It's difficult to get face to face with an older baby or toddler for a sustained period and remain relaxed physically – unless you share a bath together! Sit your toddler at one end of the tub and sink down in the water so that your heads are at an equal height. Then play sound games and singing, float ducks to one another, blow bubbles and take it in turns to ask each other questions, waiting for an answer to come as a babble of syllables or in a splash of the hand. All of these games encourage your baby's language development.

757
Copy play

It's liberating for your baby to lead a play session and relaxing for you to stop controlling for once and instead begin to observe and to copy. Put your baby down and watch him. Echo his movements and noises, connecting with the physical language of the body. Let your baby set the agenda.

758
Calming foot massage

Babies adore having their legs and feet rubbed; they find it calming and enjoy the communication. Practise for a few minutes after changing a nappy or before bed, using a little grapeseed oil.

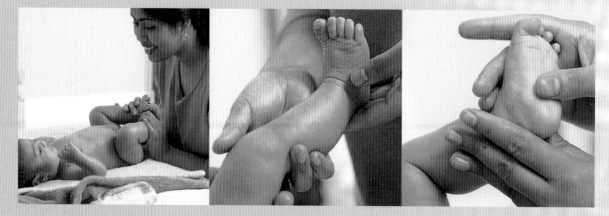

1 **Place your baby** on her back and sit in front of her. Wrap your hands around both her feet and gently stroke them with your fingers.

2 **Wrap your hand** around her leg and sweep down to the ankle. Repeat with the other hand, alternating strokes to make a flowing movement.

3 **Rest the heel** of the foot on your palm and sweep your thumb up the sole and out in a T shape. Repeat all the strokes on the other leg and foot.

759
Clear a space
Infant-play researchers report that it's impossible to engage fully with babies in a cluttered space – they get distracted by objects. Removing everything but you and your baby from a room makes space for you to engage with each other, which is profoundly relaxing.

760
Make some dad time
A study reported in *Early Child Development and Care* found that if fathers massaged their babies for around 15 minutes every day before the baby's bedtime over the period of a month, the dads became better able to relax around and interact with their babies.

761
Places to relax with baby
Baby-friendly places to relax transform a stressful day with a young child. Adopt a café with a toy corner and comfy sofas or that tolerates food-chucking toddlers. Some expansive galleries and museums accommodate crawling babies well (check changing exhibitions for baby appeal) and help you to keep in touch with the real world. Churches are a quiet, tolerant place to feed. Bathe in the peaceful vibes.

762
Find a massage class
Learn to calm your baby and make friends – what's not to like? Massage enhances the way babies interact with parents, makes them less fussy and more sociable and can establish sleeping and waking routines.

763
Get a massage yourself
Being home on your own with a baby can be spirit-crushing. Have someone babysit while you go for a massage, accompanied by relaxing music. A study in *Psychiatry* found that even brief massage sessions with music stimulated more symmetrical brain activity (asymmetry, with greater activity in the right frontal lobe, is linked to depression). Other studies back up the power of massage to lift anxiety in depressed mothers.

764
Baby yoga
Studies show that baby yoga brings about a more engaged and interactive parent-child relationship that leaves you both feeling calmer. Yoga also seems to help babies sleep better and can relieve digestive discomfort, too. Most of all, it's a fun way for you to relax together. Although it is possible to learn the postures and movement sequences from a book, nothing beats the inspiration and encouragement of a live teacher and session.

765
Post-travel yoga
We tend to restrict our babies' bodies with hours spent in buggies and car seats. When you reach your destination, stretch out his limbs with this baby-yoga routine.

Unstrap your baby and lie him on his back on a lambskin or other soft surface. Take his hands in your hands and slowly open out his arms in line with his shoulders, then cross them over his chest and hold for a moment. Repeat, gradually making the stretches wider and alternating the cross of the arms.

Bring the soles of your baby's feet together and press them towards his groin, allowing the knees to flop

The calming qualities of camomile can help to soothe a colicky baby.

outwards. Hold, stretch the legs, and repeat a few times.

Bring your baby's right hand to his left knee, hold, then pull away to a wide diagonal stretch. Repeat a few times, then swap sides, taking his left hand and right knee to meet.

766
Get out and about

To stay relaxed with a baby, it's essential to get out. Put your baby in a sling and use walks to forge links with other parents – a good way to explore the unsettling feelings parenthood brings. See if there's a local parent-and-baby group to give you and your child a place to see how other babies and parents work.

767
In or out?

Infants carried face-out in slings were found to be more active – and interactive – in a study reported in *Early Child Development and Care* than those carried face-in. Vary how you carry your baby to keep her relaxed. When she's teasy, moving her to face your chest can ease her into sleep, whereas a bored baby might stop crying if turned out to face the world.

Carrying your baby close to your body is comforting for him and makes getting around a breeze.

768
Focus on the bigger picture

When life crashes around you, hold the thought that you won't be doing this forever – visualize your child aged five or 18 – blanking out the problems these ages bring!

769
Baby photo therapy

Remind yourself of how special this person is to counter the monotony and frustration of daily battles over teeth-cleaning, washing and feeding. Get out the baby pictures and wallow.

770
A new start

To stay relaxed, shed control. You no longer rule when you sleep, dress or leave the house, where you go and with whom. To resist is futile and stressing. Regard this as a new beginning when relationships, living space and work are up for re-negotiation. Feeling out of control can be liberating – as can not having time to worry about yourself!

771
Experts do your head in

Baby manuals are a great resource, but if you find they contradict each other or pressurize you to conform to a norm you're uncomfortable with, stop reading and trust your instincts.

Time with the children

Many parents feel that children are not enjoying as relaxed a childhood as they did. Today's children are in full-time education earlier, tested more and urged to compete with others for school places. Free time may be spent playing electronic games or being herded from one activity to another because of worry about traffic and crime. Time for relaxed hanging out as a family is also cut into as parents work long hours. Here are ways to reclaim time together.

Quality father-and-son time is an invaluable part of a boy's development.

772

The simple things

A 2007 survey into how childhood has changed in a generation in the UK found that parents fear children are missing out on activities they enjoyed. Why not try the following pusuits?

- Board games played as a family.
- Traditional playground games like skipping, hop-scotch and chasing.
- Day trips to the seaside.
- Brownie Guides and Cub Scouts.
- Visiting museums.
- Religious and community festivals.
- Freedom to play outside.
- Storytelling and reading sessions.

773

Dads matter

An enquiry into a UNICEF study showing that British children suffer the lowest quality of life in the developed world pinpoints the role dads play in children's happiness – particularly between fathers and sons. Men's parenting encourages risk-taking that promotes a relaxed independence. This positively affects boys' behaviour and educational attainment, and buffers children against risk-taking in adolescence. Plan dad and son days out to relax in daring ways, perhaps climbing trees, racing go-carts or sailboarding.

774

Do stuff together

The Joseph Rowntree Foundation found that three million parents of under-14s in the UK work weekends. This stresses relations, depriving children of time with parents (with a negative impact on educational attainment and emotional development). When you can, plan activities that allow you to enjoy time together, preferably outdoors – camping is especially effective at forcing families to collaborate.

775

Eat as a family

Children of families who eat around a table each day tend to enjoy better educational attainment. Having a set family mealtime engenders security in anxious children, deters fussy eating and offers a place to discuss worries and triumphs, and to learn how to look at others, listen and share. Just plan it in.

776

Reduce choice

Giving children too much choice – from cereals to how to spend a day – can lead to anxiety. If your child is a fussy eater, explore what happens if you eat meals without serving a choice (you have to eat it, too). Have the willpower to keep this up. Being a relaxed adult is about taking the responsibility for decision-making.

Spending time relaxing together helps to reduce family stress.

780
Quality time?

If you spend hours away from your child, try not to shoehorn formal or educational activities into your time together: brain-stimulating puzzles, piano practice, language learning. It may be the smaller, informal things you do together – the quantity time – that mean more to your child and give him space to chat about issues. Try to do mundane stuff, too, like loading the washing machine, washing up or grading the recycling.

781
Do nothing

Have a family day when nothing is planned, but you stay together and agree on how to spend the time.

782
Consider childcare

A study by the National Institute of Child Health and Human Development suggests that some children who spend long hours in a nursery (over 30 a week) under the age of four and a half (and especially from birth to 54 months) are more likely to be aggressive or anxious. Some experts believe such negative behaviour may in part result from parents working longer, later hours. Could you opt for part-time working before your child enters full-time education?

777
Get cosy

Watch a film together. Try an *animé* from Japan's Studio Ghibli, uplifting children's films that explore themes like loneliness and the power of the natural and spirit worlds. *My Neighbour Totoro* is a good start.

778
Act silly

Make time for craziness in your family. Recite nonsense poems, make up rhymes, perform silly walks and play childish games; let the youngest be king for the day. Subverting norms relaxes you to play with the boundaries of conventional behaviour, which can help kids to let off steam.

779
Apple bobbing

Because an apple is 20–25 per cent air, it floats in water, lending itself to silly games. (Put down lots of newspaper or play outdoors.) Fill a washing-up bowl with water and float apples on the surface. Put on waterproof aprons and tie back long hair, then try to pick up the apples with your teeth.

783
Cuddle your child

Loving touch cools aggression. In a study of preschoolers, those from a touchy culture (France) were less aggressive than those from low-touch America (results replicated in adults). After massage, preschoolers in a study from *Early Child Development and Care* were calmer and did better in puzzles than those who were read stories. Carry on cuddling.

784
Put your child in charge

Once a week, spend an hour doing what your child wants to do: baking, playing football, watching a movie.

785
TV-free zone

Kids with TVs in their rooms have more trouble getting to sleep. Resist peer pressure and ban bedroom screens (computer monitor, games consoles and TV). Offer books instead.

786
Keep on stroking

As your child grows, don't drop a bedtime massage – even if it's just stroking hands or rubbing shoulders. In studies, preschoolers massaged found it easier to fall asleep and had better sleep patterns. Their overall behaviour improved as a result.

787
Fun yoga for kids

Children enjoy yoga with a story. Imagine visiting countries and being the animals and plants there. Keep it fast-moving to prevent boredom.
Cat (or tiger, lion or puma). On hands and knees, inhale, look up and dip the back. Exhale and arch your back, relaxing the head. Repeat, wagging your tail and moving around.
Snake (rattlesnake, mamba or cobra). Lie on your tummy, your hands under the shoulders, elbows down. Then wriggle and hiss.
Butterfly Sit tall, knees bent, soles of your feet joined. Hold your feet and flap your knees like wings. Use this to travel between places and poses.
Quiet sitting Sit quietly or lie down and listen to parts of your inner body.

Cover yourself with a blanket if you are cold. Hide a treat under a child's blanket to enjoy after the session.

788
Foster creativity

Use an under-used dining room as an area for children to dabble with clay and paint, scissors and paper. Ignore the mess: maybe clear it once a month to let children do long-term projects or experiment with media.

789
Ban perfection

Resist the urge to finish a child's creation or give meaning to her scribbles. Let her put in eyes where she wants and gain self-esteem from being trusted to accomplish a task.

Take a back seat sometimes and let your child choose an activity.

790
Trace your family tree
Get children to trace their roots to tie them in with family heritage. This is a good excuse to restart neglected family relationships.

791
Talk about the family
American research in 2006 shows that pre-teens who know where they fit in the family from family stories score highly for self-esteem and deal better with emotional stress in adulthood. Recall your childhood, past jobs, celebrations and when things went wrong. Get children to make a book of family tales and jokes.

792
Grow your own apple tree
Eat apples (of different varieties), and grow the pips, one of the easiest of seeds to sprout. Do this in winter. Compete to see whose grows largest. **Soak the pips** for a day. Fill two small pots with non-peat compost, packing it down. Put seeds in and cover with 1cm of compost. Water. Place the pots outside for eight weeks in a relatively exposed place. **At the start of spring**, bring in the pots. Put in a propagator (or large glass jars covered with a glass saucer or cling film). Site in a warm, light place and keep watered. Wait 3–8 weeks for germination. **Different varieties** will germinate and grow at different rates. When each plant is big enough to handle, "prick out" from the pot by the leaves and transfer to a 7-cm pot filled with compost. Water. When it outgrows its container, pot into one a little larger (in the winter).

793
Making a peg doll
This is a simple, fun activity to do together, suitable for children from about three years upwards, and the results can be stunning.

- Scraps of fabric: silk, tulle, netting
- Pack of wooden dolly clothes pegs
- Assorted ribbons
- Metallic embroidery silk
- Non-toxic glue
- 2–3 artificial flowers
- Felt-tipped pens

  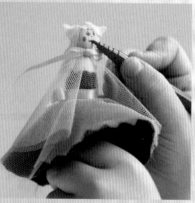

1 Cut the scraps of fabric to make a dress and cape shape. Wrap them around the "body" of the peg and tie with ribbon at the "neck" to fix.

2 Snip strands of the embroidery silk to make hair. Stick to the head with a little glue. Dry, standing the doll upright, then trim into style.

3 Disassemble the flowers. Choose a bloom for a hat. When the hair is dry, glue on the hat at a jaunty angle. Leave to dry, then draw on a face.

Calming children

It's more common than you think for children to exhibit anxiety, from refusing to let go of you to tantrumming at the thought of the dark or school. Research from the University of Manchester suggests that finding ways to help your child manage anxiety and become more confident can be more helpful than relying on health professionals.

794
Teaching kids to chill out

Children learn how to cope with stress by observing you. Let this motivate you to find better ways to deal with anger and stress. Children also tend to stay resilient if you talk over how different family members deal with problems.

795
For the serious child

Children who are a little too serious benefit from taking the Australian Bush Flower Essence Little Flannel Flower. It also helps young children to connect with the spiritual realm.

796
Making lavender bags

Grow lavender for its antidepressant properties and to lull older children asleep when under a pillow. Lavender calms and eases muscle tension.

Lavender bushes
Large bowl
Remnants of fabric and fabric scissors
Ribbon

Pick lavender stems once the flowers harden and fade. Strip the flowers from the stems into a bowl.
Cut out fabric circles (wrong-side up) using the bowl to draw around. Put lavender in the circles.
Gather the edges of the circle and tie with a length of ribbon to secure.

797
Chill-out music

If soothing music can quell the anxieties of infants awaiting surgery – with those exposed to lullabies leaving hospital an average three days earlier than those who didn't in one study – it may also be effective when played at home. Put on the second, slow movement of Mozart's symphonies or Bach's Brandenburg Concerto quietly to cover stressful times such as homework sessions.

798
Anxious tummy

Data from Bristol University shows that many children with a persistent tummy ache have anxious parents. Tackle your own stressors promptly.

799
Helpful herbs

The Chinese herbal remedy *Xia Ku Cao* (known as self heal) calms "liver fire", said to cause hyperactivity and tantrums. Add 30g to 750ml water, and reduce to 500ml by boiling. Cool and give your child half a cup, diluted with water or juice, each day.

800
Homeopathic advice

Different children react to the challenges of life in different ways. You may find it helpful to take your child to meet a homeopath, who will help you to understand your child's coping style and identify a remedy. For example, a child with a Calc. carb constitution is likely to express anxiety in stubbornness and independence, having a strong need to finish tasks and disliking change. A Pulsatilla child is more needy and has a fear of being left alone.

801
Calming movement

Research in the *Journal of Bodywork and Movement Therapies* found that adolescents with Attention Deficit Hyperactivity Disorder (ADHD)

Being active boosts feelings of happiness and wellbeing.

had reduced anxiety, daydreaming, inappropriate emotions and hyperactivity after t'ai chi classes.

802
Figures of eight

Kinesiologists suggest making figures of eight with the body to integrate the right and left sides of the brain and to restore equilibrium at times of stress. Play elephants, your arms as trunks weaving in a figure of eight. If your child loves drawing, have him compose a pattern from interlinking sideways eights, or draw large eights outside with chalk.

803
Get moving

Any exercise restores brain chemicals that promote positivity, including switching on dopamine, a chemical that aids self-control. If your child hates contact sport, try gymnastics, trampolining, yoga or cycling.

804
Massage your kids

Children who are extremely active seem to display less anxious or fidgety behaviour after being massaged, show a number of studies. Afterwards, they seem more able to focus for longer on tasks and appear to be happier.

805
Speak up

When your child is being positive and brave, give him lots of praise and positive atention. Try to ignore him when he's not acting so great. Engineer chances for success, when he can show he's good at sport or music, for example.

806
Sleep and good food

Anxious children may need more sleep: if the body is always vigilant, it burns energy and needs to recover. Also, give your child small, frequent meals of vitamin- and mineral-rich fruit and vegetables, energy-giving whole grains, nuts and seeds, fish and meat, water, milk and yogurt. Avoid caffeinated drinks and processed foods. Ask a dietician specializing in children's anxiety for advice.

807
Chew slowly

Teach children to eat slowly by your own example, putting down cutlery and chewing well. This makes for a more relaxed digestive system.

808
Fish oils

A fish-oil and evening primrose oil supplement may calm behaviour. In a study in childcare centres in Durham, UK, a fish-oil supplement with evening primrose oil boosted bonding, concentration and language skills, and reduced bad behaviour.

809
Try meditation

Being aware of your thoughts can reduce anxiety and build resilience, suggest studies. Meditation stimulates activity in the front left of the brain: the part that is active in

Evening primrose oil helps to calm.

positive people with low anxiety. Look for child meditation sessions at yoga centres, or try the ideas below.

810

Worry glasses

Buy two pairs of fun glasses from a toy shop. Call one pair worry glasses. Ask your child to put them on and talk about a situation he is anxious about, perhaps a test or new teacher. Ask him to put on the second pair and see how the situation is with non-worry glasses. What is most likely? How might others see things? Help him to assess the risks.

811

Bedtime meditation

After a story, lie down with your child and close your eyes. Ask her to watch her breathing and tell you what she sees in her head. Ask her how often images change and then to imagine each thought is in a balloon, and to let go of the ribbon and watch it being blown away. Then watch the next balloon drift away, too.

812

Safe place visualization

Ask your child to sit with her eyes closed and imagine opening a door and walking into a flower-filled garden. Ask her who is on the bench in a cosy corner – someone she loves and trusts. Have her hug the person

Bite-sized nutritious treats keep energy levels steady, helping to quell anxiety.

and sit next to her. What does the person say to make her happy? Then ask her to leave, keeping the key so she can return. Another person who loves her is standing outside the door ready to hug her. Ask her who it is.

813

Cranial sacral therapy

A therapist observes your child, then lays on his hands to "listen" to her. Patients report that anxious infants relax more afterwards, behave better and cope better with stress.

814

Cognitive therapy

Working with a therapist can help a child to challenge the anxious way in which he appraises situations and recognize that his feelings aren't borne out by the riskiness of an event. Once the child makes a more realistic assessment of the world, he is desensitized by gradual exposure to stress. Contact the British Association of Behavioural and Cognitive Psychotherapies at www.babcp.org.uk.

Retreating within

Sometimes, the best way to relax is to get away and spend time alone. When we can find a still point amid the onslaught of commitments, deadlines and obligations, we can recollect over-stretched energies and dip into our well of inner resources, nurturing ourselves so we are ready to take on the world again. Checking in with ourselves equips us to emerge with greater compassion and more energy.

815
Yearly check-in

When you wake up thinking "Is this all there is?", it's time to book some "me" time. Have at least a day and a night away on your own, holing up somewhere other than home where you don't have to make polite chit-chat or do anything for anyone. Take long walks, deep baths, eat well, get

Choose a retreat where you can pursue an interest or learn a new skill.

lots of sleep and avoid shopping, drinking and gossiping – activities that distract you from yourself.

816
Contemplate your life

Use a retreat to reflect on life as you currently live it. List the year's most rewarding and most challenging events. How do they reflect on your light and dark corners; what can you learn? Who supported you this year; which friendships fell away and which are worth nurturing? How could you renegotiate relationships for the better? Throughout, think not about what you want, but what you need, and aim to go home with an awareness of your blessings.

817
Keeping silent

Watch what happens when you stay silent: your concentration is more focused and you feel more awake yet aware of your inner voice shouting.

Make it a habit – turn off the phone, TV and music as well as your voice, and observe how eventually the loud mouth within becomes more muted and you start to intuit what Quakers call the "small still voice".

818
Share silence

Being silent with others is deeply reassuring, helping you to appreciate the different qualities of silence that accompany prayer, meditation and everyday tasks. Join a meditation group or a silent retreat, maybe with a holy order that has a vow of silence.

819
Pulling in the senses

Sit or lie quietly and close your eyes. Let your hands and feet relax. Withdraw awareness from your eyes and feel them quieten and lie heavy in their sockets, then withdraw your interaction from the world with your mouth. Let your tongue rest on your palate and lips relax. What can you smell? Let it go, drawing awareness inwards. Observe noises around you, near and far and from left and right. Detach from their meaning, so that they become patterns of sound. Let these go, too, and draw your sense of hearing within. Finally, be aware of sensations on your face and skin. Disengage and draw this awareness within, to your heart. Dwell inside for 5–10 minutes.

820

Religious retreats

These are safe places to be silent if quietness brings pain, anger or guilt. Experienced people can guide you through prayer and meditation.

821

Crafty retreats

If your way of retreating from stress is to pursue a craft, there are retreats around the world for you. As well as quilting, writing or playing the harp, you'll find beautiful scenery, walks, campfires, good food and often complementary therapies, from massage to yoga classes.

822

Spa treat

A day at a spa can serve as a retreat if the therapists are sensitive and the surroundings inspiring. Look for places where you can escape to sit on a hill or bathe outdoors between treatments. Or find a spa centre that has an outdoor pool set in beautiful surroundings, or where you can have treatments in tee-pees or pavilions open to the elements so that you can gaze down at the sea or onto a still pond.

Enjoy the liberating feeling of bathing in stunning surroundings.

823
Take a long walk

A pilgrimage is a walking retreat, traditionally to a place of worship, that calms the body through repeated activity and frees the mind to reflect on the spirit. It's reassuring to follow a trail marked out over thousands of years. Look into the pilgrimage route to Santiago De Compostela in Spain, a thriving retreat used since before the 11th century.

824
Mother and baby retreats

Some orders of nuns have mother and baby retreats. The nuns look after the baby so you can walk, sleep, read or attend a service of worship and discussions about the spiritual dimensions of motherhood. These are very special, nurturing spaces.

825
Read haiku

Take the works of Japanese writer Matsuo Basho (1644–94) on retreat. He composed many haiku, or verses, on pilgrimages or while sitting still in the *basho* hut to which he retreated. In the 17 syllables of a haiku, he gives a visionary, fleeting glimpse of the present moment in nature, overlaid with the melancholy of flawed human pasts and future dreams that drag us from this intense connection with now and with nature.

Spiritual nourishment

Organized religion is so much in retreat that few people under 50 have a memory of what it is to live as part of a religious community with shared beliefs and values. What does remain is a sense that we have a spiritual element within us that demands to be explored if we are to lead a good, relaxed and happy life. Seeking to fulfil that sacred part of your being can bring about peace and a fulfilling sense of connection and compassion.

826
Letting go

Faith is about letting go, about feeling rather than seeking to rationalize or understand with the intellect. Allow the earthly impossibilities of a virgin birth, of a reality beyond time and space or of the sound of one hand clapping to allow you to circumvent ingrained thoughts and behaviour patterns. We are not supposed to glimpse God or heaven; both are unknowable, and there are no answers, only questions that make us look at how we inhabit our world.

827
It's all about you

Reflect on who you are inside to find the spark of the divine within. The Prophet Mohammed said that to know God you must first gain knowledge about yourself.

828
Shopping around

Those of us who aren't spiritually embedded can feel stressed and isolated by our search for faith, as we assess the various systems, sub-sects, leaders and gurus in search of the perfect fit. But spirituality isn't a shopping experience. The Tibetan Buddhist teacher Trungpa Rinpoche warns of the dangers of "spiritual materialism": it allows us to create a "religious" ego that is eager for learning but creates a barrier to faith.

829
Slipping from the grasp

Consider the following quotation from the anonymous 14th-century author of a key spiritual road map, *The Cloud of Unknowing*: "By love he can be caught and held, but by thinking never."

Look deep within to discover the power of prayer.

834
Soak in silence

The German theologian and mystic Meister Eckhart (*c.*1260–*c.*1328) wrote "Nothing in all creation is so like God as silence." Consider this as you sit and quietly contemplate in a place of worship or wonder.

835
A first prayer

People from many denominations find this Russian Orthodox prayer a good place to start praying: "Lord Jesus Christ, son of God, have mercy on me, a sinner." When repeated under the breath it echoes like a bassline to which life's melody plays over, and leads us to God's

830
Light incense

To create a state conducive to prayer, light frankincense or sandalwood incense, or to increase compassion place 4 drops of essential oil of rose in a vaporizer.

831
Try a prayer

Prayer is not about asking for things. It's about pulling away from the head to the heart, an act thought to lead us towards union with the divine. In Islam prayer is regarded as a ladder by which we ascend to God.

832
Opening the door

Sit in a place of worship or natural beauty. Close your eyes, hands on the thighs, palms facing up. See your heart opening like a door and sit with this openness for a few minutes. If this level of receptivity feels scary, leave the door only slightly ajar. Close it before returning to the world.

833
Give it up

When you are in a receptive state, try reciting the un-denominational prayer, "Grant me a pure heart".

Burn essential oil of rose to enhance feelings of compassion.

command to, "Rejoice evermore. Pray without ceasing. In every thing give thanks" (1 *Thessalonians* 5: 16–18).

836

Do something practical

Find a practical focus to explore religion. Observe fast days of your faith or one you are drawn to – Lent, Ramadan, Yom Kippur. Testing yourself and aligning with others helps you to feel unity and brings a sense of euphoria that in some faiths links to a higher state of consciousness. Being hungry is also said to soften and open the heart to those less fortunate. (Avoid if you are pregnant or have a medical condition.)

Spend time in a remote, holy place and experience the incredible serenity and sense of faith.

837

Holy places

Visit places where people with faith have lived. Sit and be attentive: the faith can be tangible. Especially numinous are places where hermits lived, often sites of inhospitable remoteness and uncompromising beauty at the edge of the world, where you gaze to infinity. Visit holy islands such as Skellig Michael off the coast of Ireland, or sacred mountain-tops, such as Mount Sinai in Egypt.

838

Explore exuberant worship

Waving hands, singing, chanting and moving helps some experience a divine connection. If this appeals, investigate West Indian or African Christian congregations, the Sufi tradition of Islam or the Hindu *bhakti* path of devotion to Krishna.

839

Try ecstatic postures

The body can adopt postures to express humility or connection, or to help you ascend to the divine. Kneel to pray; prostrate yourself if you feel the force or learn the movements of Muslim daily prayers.

840

Anjali (offering) mudra

A mudra is a position that brings about an inner state. Try the gesture of prayer, welcome and humility sacred to Christianity, Hinduism and Buddhism by joining the palms

at your chest. Feel your fingers against their opposite partners and the heels of your hands anchoring your palms. Press the thumbs into the breastbone to make the connection with your heart as your fingers point to the heavenly realm. (To sense how centring this is, swerve them off-centre for a moment.) You might fan your fingers as a sign of opening up to divine love, cup your palms like a bud in a symbol of potential or touch your fingertips briefly to your forehead to connect head and heart.

841

Keep your sacred day

Whichever day of the week is holy in your tradition, observe its sacred practices. Keep it as a day of rest, reflection and devotion to family by cooking traditional foods, lighting candles, saying holy words over food and giving thanks before bed.

842

Spiritual community

The word *religion* derives from the Latin verb meaning "to tie in" or bind together. All religions teach us to look within, but to do so with others, and to use what we learn to better the lives of those around us. Being religious makes you part of a greater body and this is stress-busting. In studies, people who state that they have faith feel happier and more satisfied with life and emotionally stable than those without – a 1999 study even found that attending religious services added seven years to life.

843

Do service

The Christian monastic tradition teaches us to be still through prayer and humble through service. This twin approach of balancing inner and outer work resembles the yogic path of inner transformation. It helps us to develop an equanimity that equips us to face challenges. While you explore your inner path, do some public good works.

844

Attend a religious service

It's all very well being "spiritual", but it's not until you take the plunge and worship in a congregation that you gain the destressing benefits of a religious life.

5 Unwinding at times of stress

It's important to relieve muscular tension, clear the mind and lift the spirits during anxious times. The top causes of anxiety, apart from work, were outlined by two American psychologists in 1967. The top five are the death of a partner, divorce, separation, imprisonment and loss of a loved one. Such personal anxiety can reduce life expectancy by up to four years. Other stressors include financial and health worries. Current research exposes how we stress over "enjoyable" events such as vacations, national holidays and family festivities. Here are ways to cope with tricky times, from dealing with debt to preparing mind and body for a party. Plus, there are tips on how to avoid that favourite prop of the stressed, smoking.

Easing money worries

Research links financial stress to depression, high blood pressure, insomnia, fatigue, digestive ailments and overeating. Up to half of those polled by Mental Health America in 2006 had financial stress, which a study at Ohio State University found is more likely to cause depression than the loss of a loved one. Here are ways to ease worries that don't include the lottery: in a study, lottery winners and paraplegics were equally happy a year on from their life-changing event.

845
Plan your spending
If you don't know where your salary goes, write a budget. Record income, then outgoings: housing, bills (gas, electricity, water, phones, internet, TV, taxes), debt payments, food, travel (including car costs), savings, insurance, holidays and going out. Many seem to think all our income is destined for the latter! Where can you save money, and where do you need to spend more? Update it each month to assuage money worries.

846
Get your finances in order
Not making a credit-card payment because you forgot to open the bill leads to unnecessary costs as well as unnecessary stress – and even blacklisting from future loans. Create files for credit card and bank statements, tax matters and household bills, then put aside one evening a month to check and file bills and statements. Setting up direct-debit payments will ensure you never miss a deadline again.

847
Consolidate
Put overspending worries in one place by moving debts to one 0 per cent interest credit card. Then cut it up and watch the debt decrease as you pay it off each month.

848
Just say no
Avoid store cards, perhaps the most expensive form of easy credit. Cut them up now. Instead, try to pay for most things with cash.

849
Stop grinding your teeth
People who worry about financial stress but avoid doing anything about it seem more prone to dental disease than those who grasp the nettle, suggests a study in *Journal of*

Rationalize your filing system to remove unnecessary stress.

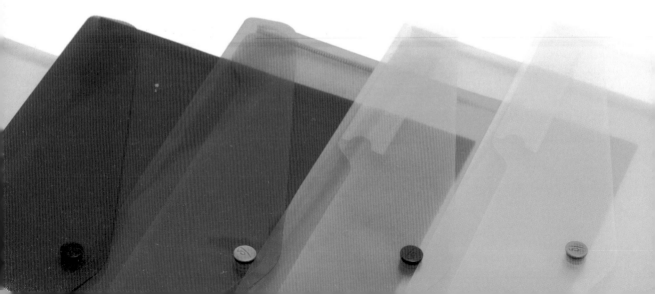

Try Feng Shui: nurture a money plant in the financial corner of your home.

Peridontology, which found finances to be the only stressor that had this effect (marital and job stress didn't figure so highly). Do something about your accounts if only for the sake of your teeth!

850

Buy just what you can afford

Save up for something. Savouring the anticipation of being able to afford a luxury item is more stress-busting than worrying about how you are going to pay off the ensuing credit-card debt.

851

Homeopathy help

If anxiety levels rise when you think about money and you spend hours pouring over bank statements or doing frantic calculations, take a dose of the homeopathic remedy Ars.Alb 30, and go and do something enjoyable instead.

852

Crystal protection

Placing cleansing, protective crystal citrine in a house's money corner (the farthest back left point from the front door) is said in Feng Shui to attract prosperity. Try putting a money plant in this position, too.

853

Make a will

It may seem stressful to think about death, but it gives a perspective on the tiny stressors that assault us each day. It's especially reassuring if you have children, but are unmarried, to map out their future without you. Wander in graveyards as you ponder the issues. Thoughts about death force us to appreciate the miracle of life and free us to live it more fully.

854

Do it now

Stop prevaricating. Money worries won't go away. Talk to a financial adviser or debt counsellor, or for free advice call the Consumer Credit Counselling Service (www.cccs.co.uk).

Coping with hard times

Whatever your stressor – relationship crisis, illness, grief – paying attention to basic relaxation strategies can help your body and mind to counter the stress hormones that bring on panic and palpitations, and deplete your nervous system of the vitamins and minerals it requires to function well.

855

Avoid anxiety

Stop reading the newspaper or watching TV news reports to avoid other people's wars and tragedy impinging on your own burdens for a while. Think about the wise words of Benjamin Franklin (1706–90), "Do not anticipate trouble, or worry about what may never happen. Keep in the sunlight."

856

Become an observer

Yoga urges us to cultivate a detached awareness – to become someone who watches and so does not get submerged beneath sanity-drowning waves of passion and judgement. Observe situations objectively. You might imagine yourself in the balcony of a theatre watching a play unfold far below.

857

Watch your diet

A poll by Mental Health America in 2006 found that women were more likely to eat as a way of coping with stress. If this is you, avoid mood-stressing foods that don't provide nutrients to keep the nervous system functioning – that includes sugary treats, caffeine and confectionery.

858

Eat well

Some foods are particularly helpful at bringing relief from symptoms of stress. At difficult times, build your diet around colour-rich fruit and vegetables, oily fish, whole grains, and sources of B vitamins (chicken, avocados and bananas in particular).

859

Destressing arguments

To stop blood pressure and heart rate spiking in arguments, stay calm and in control by separating facts

Avocados contain destressing B vitamins.

from emotions. State what the other person did to upset you without exaggerating or judging – "You didn't show up for the meeting we had arranged." Then coolly set out the negative effects of this – "I had taken time off work and now I'll miss a deadline." End with a request for help – "How can we get back on track?"

860

Depersonalize insults

When you express to someone how much they've hurt you, resist the urge to lash out and minimize the potential for more conflict by using first-person statements, such as "I feel frustrated when you do that because…". Conversely, if praising, use the second person "you". This sounds over-simple, but works.

861

Be inclusive

A study in *Psychological Science* found that people who say "we" most in arguments come up with the best solutions for both concerned parties. Those who say "you" a lot tend to be more stressed, negative and critical.

862

Win win

During a dispute, think about how both parties can emerge from a misunderstanding or conflict with dignity and a positive outcome.

863

Flower empowering

Take the Australian Bush Flower Essence Red Suva Frangipani to soothe raw, painful emotions when a relationship is ending or going through a difficult time.

864

Soften your gaze

At times of conflict notice whether your eyes have hardened or are staring. Soften and widen your gaze. In yoga this is believed to relax the frontal lobes of the brain, calm the mind and relax the diaphragm, making deep breathing more easy.

865

Release body tension

To reach areas of stress you weren't aware of, lie down and tense the lower body. Contract your muscles, from your toes to your abdomen, and hold your breath. Release and relax. Repeat, contracting your upper body, from your fingers and chest to your shoulders and face. Hold, then release. Repeat on any areas of the body that still feel tense.

866

Talking therapy

Actively addressing painful issues can lower your stress levels. Researchers at the University of

Copenhagen found that men who talked about their infertility – whether with professionals or friends – felt that their relationship with their partner became closer as a result, bringing protection from the negative effects of stress. Those who avoided issues ratcheted up the stress and as a result felt that their marriages were less stable.

867

Love your pet

Studies of men with HIV/AIDS show that those who have a pet are much less likely to report symptoms of depression, and a group of high-powered, work-stressed New Yorkers with high blood pressure were found to reduce their blood pressure and heart rates by acquiring a pet.

868

Positive thinking

Actively dwelling on symptoms seems to magnify them, increasing our perception of pain and discomfort. Instead, try scanning your body to find areas that are free from pain: think about your nose, your toes, your skin and your hair follicles. Thinking in a positive way has the effect of attracting more positive thoughts. Imagine this positivity clumping together to form a mass that can overpower feelings of negativity.

Making room in your life for a pet provides a significant boost to wellbeing.

869

Find a support group

Online support groups can help chronic health sufferers. In a 2005 study, 74 per cent of a web-based diabetes group felt more hopeful about their health after chatting online.

870

Pain-relieving music

Slow music, with fewer than 80 beats per minute, reduces our perception of pain when listened to for at least 20 minutes, found a 2003 survey of chronic osteoarthritis sufferers. The music used in the study was Mozart's *Overture to The Marriage of Figaro* and the first movement of his *Symphony No. 40* in G minor (K550).

871

Look on the bright side

Approaching illness in a state of optimism is helpful because positivity has been shown to boost your immunity as well as lowering blood pressure.

872

Dental fear

If you fear dentists, find one who uses homeopathic remedies to calm nerves as well as deal with dental problems (they also don't use mercury). Contact the British Homeopathic Dental Association (www.bhda.co.uk).

873

Have a cuppa

Tea is the traditional British tonic for trauma. Research by University

874

Yoga for fortitude

When dealing with difficult emotions it's important to stay centred, but not too open. This yoga sequence may be helpful.

1 Kneel, sitting on your heels. Interlink the fingers, palms turned out, and stretch your arms up. Breathe, releasing the buttocks.

2 Still kneeling, widen the knees and, keeping your buttocks down, walk your hands forwards and relax your head to the floor. Quieten your mind.

3 Sit upright, resting your palms. Close your eyes and focus on your breathing. Sense the firmness and resolve in the pose.

College London from 2006 suggests that tea indeed helps by lowering levels of the stress hormone cortisol. Make it in a pot: you get a better cup of tea and there's more to go around.

875
Homeopathy for grief
Although these are available over the counter, after a loss seek treatment from a professional homeopath.
• Aconite when you feel numb, disbelieving or have a sense of unreality about what has happened.
• Ignatia for acute grief with much crying, sighing, emotional outbursts and a constant lump in the throat.
• Nat.Mur if your loss was some time ago, but you remain stuck in sadness.

876
Herbal help
The herbal tincture made from oats (*Avena sativa*) is an antidepressant and restorative nerve tonic good for those who have to deal with a prolonged period of stress, such as nursing a sick relative. Place 10–30 drops in a cup of water and drink 2–3 times a day.

877
Extreme activity
Body-breaking activity can help to cope with loss: climbing a mountain, training for a marathon, landscaping a garden or building a wall can numb pain and provide purposeful focus.

Immersing yourself in a creative pursuit can be an effective way to channel grief.

878
The power of art
A body of evidence supports the healing and empowering nature of art projects to ease the stress of those who face illness and grief – being creative is a life-affirming way to focus thoughts and activities in a mourning period. It is especially helpful to get together with family or friends to make a piece of art – a quilt of memories perhaps, to which each person contributes a square.

879
Feel the *saudade*
Brazilian music raises this hard-to-translate emotion to a high art. *Saudade* might be explained as a longing for something that one no longer has, yet which might be restored. The joy of remembering is savoured despite the rush of intense sadness, and emotional growth comes with accepting fate, making this melancholic emotion peculiarly uplifting. It's easier heard than explained: listen to the bossa nova of Joao Gilberto and Anton Carlos "Tom" Jobim and see if it helps you to trace the joy in your loss.

880
Tonglen meditation
The following Tibetan Buddhist meditation encourages us to connect with the suffering of others and, by arousing our compassion, to transform it into positivity. This is best practised when you are feeling strong and healthy. You can use this technique on a wider scale to send relief to all those who are suffering around the globe.

Think of your loved one's pain or suffering. As you inhale, breathe it in – you might visualize it as a dark cloud. Absorb the pain, feeling it inside your heart.

Now transform those sensations within your heart; feel them purify and soften, and dissolve into love and joyousness. As you breathe out, send out those healing loving sensations to your loved one to relieve her distress. Imagine them as rays of light that soothe and lift her, bringing peace.

Pressure busting

Cramming before an exam or preparing for a driving test – and having to live with the black cloud of teenagers or partners who are doing so – can be trying, but exhilarating, since such testing times tend to be intense but short-lived. Here are ways to cope.

Exercise your heart and lungs to boost your brain power.

881
Alternate activities
After a period of intense study, get some exercise that works the heart and lungs. Go for a jog, have a skip, bounce on a trampoline or do work around the house or garden. Aim to work for 10–20 minutes at a level that leaves you a bit breathless. This not only destresses, it also seems to fix facts in the brain more efficiently.

882
Be an early bird
Work at times when you feel fresh – perhaps begin early and end early. Set your default to positive when you wake by saying, "I've got a long day ahead, but I'll get lots done."

883
Timetable breaks
Break up studying into 30-minute periods, making sure you *do* work during them. When your work rate dips, it's time to take a break.

884
A relaxed space
Where do you study best? In the library, on your bed, with friends? Make this your study place. If a desk makes you shake with fear, avoid it.

885
Getting over nerves
If you're paralysed with fear about an event, think what the worst outcome could be. How likely is

this? What would you do if it happened? Write down empowering strategies to combat your fears.

886

Mark off achievements

Buy a day-by-day calendar so that you can rip off the days leading up to the big event and throw them in a bin. Some people like to blow up red balloons and keep them in their work space, popping them one by one at the end of red-letter days.

887

Reading position

Rebalance the hemispheres of the brain to bring calmness and clarity, and exercise legs made restless from inactivity. Lie on your stomach, your chin in your cupped hands. Bend the knees so the soles of the feet face up and criss-cross your feet and calves, scissoring them out and back again.

888

Eat right

When working on brain-led activities eat protein; if you want to relax afterwards, take in carbohydrates.

889

Sleep essentials

If your eyes glaze over and you read the same sentence time and again, take a 15-minute nap (set an alarm).

890

Stop making fists

Notice if you are clenching your fists. If so, turn your hands over and open out your fingers. To feel more complete, sit with your hands in *Jnana* mudra, by bringing the tips of your thumbs and index fingers together. Yoga values this closed circuit of energy for recharging inner resources. The index finger represents you as an individual, the thumb the source of life. Think about the point at which they meet.

891

Lotus breathing technique

This breathing technique balances the body's energy channels.

Sit comfortably with your spine upright and your eyes closed. Rest your hands on your knees with your palms facing upwards and your fingers loose and open like petals. Inhaling, draw your fingers and thumbs together like a flower closing at night.

Exhale, opening your left hand and imagining your breath flowing out of your left side. Inhale and close your left hand, drawing the breath up the left side of your body. Open your right hand as you exhale down the right side. Breathe in through your right side, closing your right hand. Repeat for as long as feels comfortable, alternating hands.

Lavender oil is both uplifting and relaxing.

892

Sniff relaxing oils

Place a drop of essential oil on your handkerchief. In studies, rosemary reduced anxiety and lavender increased relaxation while lessening depression. Both simultaneously boosted brain performance, and thus mental coping powers.

893

Let off steam

It's not effective to concentrate for long periods, especially if you are a perfectionist! Break up study days with tension-releasing times. Physical activity is especially stress-relieving – plan a night out dancing.

894

The night before

The day before a big day stop work by 5pm, then unwind – cook, watch a funny programme, soak in the bath and go to bed at a reasonable time.

Giving up smoking

The worst way to deal with stress is to smoke: you may feel relaxed, but smoking stresses the heart by constricting blood vessels and reduces oxygen intake, and relying on an addictive crutch brings about yet more anxiety. Nicotine is a stimulant, so giving it up results in a more relaxed body.

895
Quit worrying about health
If you give up smoking you delete all those nagging worries about harming your health. It's that easy to lift a weight off your shoulders!

896
Enlist support
People who have the support of professionals and loved ones find it easier to give up. Visit your doctor or call the NHS helpline 0800 1690 169 or visit www.gosmokefree.co.uk to find out what support is available, from nicotine replacement products to local self-help groups.

897
A problem shared...
Tell friends and family that you plan to quit, and ask for their support. Could they sponsor you to keep it up (donating the money to charity to boost feelings of wellbeing), and text messages of encouragement at random moments during the day?

Stay motivated and maintain your resolve by rewarding yourself with delicious treats.

898
Keep a diary
Before quitting, keep a tobacco-use diary for one week. Make two columns and in one list the time and place of each cigarette smoked. In the other column, list triggers (social drinking, anxiety, habit). At the end of the week, try to spot patterns. Is smoking linked with particular times, places, people and situations? Brainstorm ways to avoid these.

899
Rethink your routine
Change the circumstances that link cravings with relaxation. If you have a cigarette with coffee, switch to tea.

900
Deep breathing
Some studies suggest it is the deep breathing used when smoking that is relaxing. Breathe without inhaling deadly poisons by breathing in to a count of four. Hold your breath for four, then exhale to a count of eight. If this is hard, reduce the count to 2,2,4. Gradually extend the count, but work to the same ratio (1:1:2).

901
Alternate nostril breathing
Many quitters find that this rebalancing breathing technique counters cravings (see No. 891).

902
Stroke your ears
In a 1999 study, rubbing ear lobes or hands reduced cravings, the anxious behaviour that triggered them and, crucially, the number of cigarettes smoked. Or visit an acupuncturist who may work on the ears.

903
Homeopathic help
Homeopaths treat the cravings, irritability, constipation and insomnia caused by nicotine-withdrawal with Nux.Vom 30. Take it three times daily, or if you have an acute craving. This also removes nicotine and smoking toxins from the body.

904
Cough relief
After giving up, it is common to develop a cough as the lungs cleanse themselves. The herb coltsfoot (*Tussilago farfara*) is an excellent cough remedy. Take 30 drops in a cup of water twice daily until the cough clears. (Avoid in pregnancy.)

905
Maintain your resolve
Australian Bush Flower Essence Wedding Bush can help you to keep your resolve to quit. It helps you to stick to commitments, including the one to choose a healthier lifestyle.

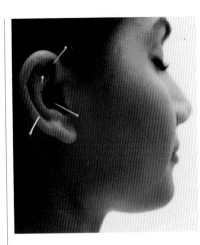

Control cravings with acupuncture.

906
Deep treats
Research suggests that women find it harder to quit than men. Motivate yourself with rewards. Perhaps a little treat every day, a middle-sized one each week and a big treat once a month. Try dark chocolate, a new book, breakfast in bed, a day at a spa or a subscription to a magazine.

907
Track your savings
Keep a record of how much money you save by not buying cigarettes: work out how many non-smoking months will fund a relaxing holiday.

908
Throat chakra meditation
Anxieties connected with the throat chakra, the energy centre concerned with communication, can manifest in smoking and other nervous oral habits like overeating. Meditating on this chakra can resolve connected issues. Sit upright, eyes closed. Watch your breathing until you feel calm. Focus on your throat. Imagine a ball of energy there getting brighter with each in-breath. Then say the throat-chakra mantra *ham* silently as you meditate for 10 minutes.

909
Chew gum
To stimulate your mouth, try chewing gum, which can also help stress-related digestive problems.

910
Start knitting
For anxious hands, join a knitting group. They welcome beginners, so don't worry if you can't knit.

911
Retreat
Look for quit-smoking retreats. Often organized by churches, these offer a blend of moral and spiritual support that can be helpful.

912
Try acupuncture
Acupuncture can be as effective as nicotine-replacement therapies. As a bonus, you lounge on a massage table and engage in talk therapy.

Relaxing vacations

Psychologists recommend that to stay relaxed and happy, we need one long break a year in which we change our surroundings and routine and try new activities. Two weeks is the recommended time, and the effects can be as positive as exercising and eating healthily. But many unable to stop work have "vacation deficit disorder", especially Americans, who take around 3–4 days' annual leave (Europeans take an average six weeks). Here are ways to get away from it all.

Dream about your ultimate destination and plan how to get there.

913
Take your full quota
People who take vacations are less likely to feel stressed, exhausted or to suffer symptoms of depression. They also reduce their risk of heart disease and tend to have a happier family life and marriages. When they return to work they report increased levels of productivity. If you don't take your full yearly quota – and increasing numbers of us don't – ask yourself why not. Would it help you to think of a holiday as a healthy lifestyle choice, like going to the gym, rather than a guilt-inducing treat? You are not failing by taking a break and they will cope in your absence.

914
Blue-sky dreaming
Where have you always wanted to go? Mount Fuji, the Antarctic, Tibet? Why haven't you got there yet? Start making a five-year plan.

915
Far from the madding crowds
If you find traffic jams and packed attractions stressful and the thought of air miles distressing, why not holiday at home? Sit in the garden reading books, eat out, visit attractions and get plenty of sex and sleep without the hassle of travel.

916
Get real
To make your holiday destressing, be realistic – children will bicker on long journeys, a baby will wake more often in strange surroundings, friends have moved on since college and traffic jams are the norm worldwide.

917
Turn that thing off
When away, switch off your mobile and stop tapping into the Blackberry. Both create an adrenalin-triggering sense of urgency that's bad-mannered and inappropriate on holiday. The most urgent thing now is repose.

918
What not to pack
- Laptop
- Schedules and spreadsheets
- Work worries
- Improving reading
- Phone charger

919
Stop negative self-talk

Counter the nagging devil on your shoulder sneering, "How's that project running while you're away?" by placing an angel of calm on the other shoulder. Make up a positive affirmation: "Everything's fine back home; I deserve to relax." If you can't think of one, ask what your best friend would advise.

920
Switch off from work mode

Change can be stressful; try to make your change of location less stressful by chilling out your itinerary. Holidaying isn't about how many sights and cities you can cram into how few days. That's your work brain thinking. Dare to spend a day doing nothing at all.

921
Do what you want

Make sure everyone on holiday gets at least a day doing something they love – trekking to ruins, making sandcastles, eating good food, lounging in the hot tub. Mothers especially may crave a break from kids and domestic chores – make sure they get it.

922
Let's get lost

Spend a day in a new town without a map or guidebook. Drop into cafés that look inviting or smell good, not because they're recommended by a book or website. When you get lost, ask or gesture for directions.

923
Change your day

Try to adapt your routine to that of the locals – take long lunches and siestas, eat late and don't try to shop, bank or sightsee when places are shut. Not adapting can lead to frustration.

Muck in with your kids on the beach and enjoy the throwback to your own childhood.

924

Blending in

Holidays in foreign parts are less stressful if you can speak enough of the language to decipher menus and understand basic directions. Follow a home-study course or attend evening classes before you go. Even better, devote your holiday to learning by taking a language break, where you sightsee, eat and shop as well as study with native speakers – what more relaxed way to learn?

925

Playtime

In our regular lives we don't get enough time to play, especially with others. As part of your holiday do something that gets you playing with new people – maybe try a circus skills workshop where you get to make a human pyramid!

Relish hassle-free camping from the comfort of a camper van.

926

Good works

Living in the heart of a place of natural beauty for a few days and giving something back to it can be a profoundly rewarding and convivial experience, if occasionally back-breaking. Look for volunteering breaks in national parks, where you get to lay paths, repair ancient walls and cut back undergrowth. Restoring beauty and order externally can help to smooth out your inner world.

927

Hit a quirky festival

Mainstream music festivals have lost their liberating edge thanks to corporate sponsorship. To find the quirky creative spirit that brought us the original free festivals of peace and self-expression, look for small, "boutique" festivals organized by and for quirky-minded individuals. They might celebrate books, clowning, folk music or all things eco, but guarantee fun camping, odd workshops, costumes and a child-friendly ethos. The more secret the event, the more exciting it will be.

928

Hire a camper van

If you're new to camping, hire a camper van. While fellow campers are struggling with poles and pegs you can, within 30 seconds of arrival, pop the top to reveal your beds, put on the kettle for a restorative cup of tea, or pull a cold beer from the fridge. Later, put up a side tent or awning in which to unload stuff (kids' car seats, food, bedding) so you can drive off for the day without struggling to pack away your life.

929

Sleep somewhere strange

Investigate innovative and surprisingly luxurious camping options – nomadic yurts, tee-pees, Mughal pavilions and painted gypsy caravans complete with horse.

930
Scary hols

Relaxing means shaking life up a bit. Why not test your insomnia by staying in a haunted house? Take a spooky tour before retiring to bed…

931
Relax up a tree

Being high is an antidote to a flat routine life, and natural highs don't come better than holidaying in a tree – right up in the canopy, suspended safely in a harness with safety ropes in a "tree boat". Begin in the afternoon with some guided tree climbing, then eat by the tree at dusk, before being tucked in for the night. As you lie there, you tune into tree time, which has therapeutic value. Alternatively, stay in a tree-top house with room to unwind and chill out.

932
Make lanterns

For relaxed evenings outdoors, you need ambient lighting. As you relax with a beer, have kids make hanging lanterns. First scrub the labels from preserve jars, then make a circlet of wire slightly larger than the neck of the jar. Slide it over the neck, then twist at each end to tighten securely. Cut another length of wire for a handle and twist onto the loops at either side of the neck. Put in a nightlight and suspend from a branch.

Escape the crowds high up in a tree-top retreat.

933
Start whittling

If you have trouble switching off, find a project that occupies your mind and your hands. Buy a lovely penknife (a vital holiday tool for opening bottles and tidying toenails) and look for an interesting piece of wood. Cut away at it to expose the spirit of the wood inside – it might be a snake, a toad or a dolphin. Observe how, gradually, the wood takes on a life of its own as you fiddle with it. Keep the finished piece as your totem of inner peace.

934
Yoga for travellers

Spend some time on planes and trains cross-legged if this is comfortable, or with your legs up on the (empty) chair in front. On long journeys, try a spot of self-exploration: put on an eye mask and ear plugs and practise looking inwards at where your breath moves in your body. Give it time – you may be surprised by the results.

935
Homeopathic travel essentials

- Arg.Nit 30 for fear of flying.
- Arnica 30, first aid for any injury and fabulous for jet lag.
- Apis 30 for insect bites and stings that cause itching and swelling.
- Ars.Alb.30 for food poisoning with vomiting and diarrhoea.
- Belladonna 30 for sunstroke, or sunburn with redness and throbbing.
- Nux.Vom 30, the best ever hangover cure.

Relaxed celebrations

If you feel stressed most days, that tension is magnified at emotionally charged times when we're expected to have fun. Christmas is especially stressful as it throws us into the lap of families we might not see often, and the pressure's on to be perfect – perfect family, perfect gifts, perfectly behaved kids. Past happy times take on extra significance too, especially for separated families with new rules and routines.

936
Look at your expectations

Lowering expectations may be the key to lowering stress. Resist the urge to be perfect and accept that family fights are unlikely to stop now.

937
Touch base

Before the chaos starts, sit quietly and ask yourself what your touchstones are. Family, worship, cooking favourite dishes? Keep them in mind as you plan schedules and negotiate priorities with others.

938
Make plans

To avoid being overwhelmed, plan what you need to do day by day as you would plan work tasks. Delegate as you would at work, too. Set kids on the wrapping – there's something charming about badly wrapped gifts covered in bows.

939
Rethink giving

Competitive gift-giving is a strain for all. Why not declare a truce and give to charity instead? Look for organizations that donate a goat or cow or a well to a village overseas.

940
Cut the clutter

If your home is full, suggest offering an exchange of skills instead: you cook and deliver a special meal; they assemble your flatpack furniture. Gifts that you really give mean more than another box of candles.

941
Services not things

To avoid more clutter, give vouchers for a destressing body service: a reflexology session, massage, haircut, or yoga or Feldenkrais posture lesson.

Homemade gifts make charming presents.

942
Loving it
No matter who you're buying for, don't invest money unless you love an item. Be discerning about what makes it off the shelf.

943
Have a homemade holiday
Don't go shopping; spend time making something to show your love – chilli oil, preserves from the hedgerow, peppermint creams, flower corsages, a fabulous tree decoration or CD compilation. Do this with the children.

944
Kate's celebration olives
These herby olives make a tasty gift that won't last long. Get a fancy jar a bit larger than the total amount of olives and with a metallic screw top.

450g drained green olives
4 garlic cloves, peeled and crushed, or to taste
freshly ground black pepper
sprinkle of caster sugar
pinch of herbes de Provence
2 tbsp good balsamic vinegar
1 tbsp extra-virgin olive oil

Place the drained olives in a bowl of water to soak for a couple of hours. Strain and pour into the large jar with the crushed garlic cloves. Season with 3–4 twists of black pepper, a sprinkling of sugar and the herbs. Pour over the vinegar and oil. Put on the lid and shake. Leave for at least two hours before tasting.

945
Keep your body relaxed
The American Physical Therapy Association (APTA) reports an increased incidence of back, neck and shoulder pain around Christmas as our lifestyles change from largely sedentary to frenzied activity, and we carry too many things in the wrong way. Ease the stress with some of the tips to reduce shoulder and back strain in Nos. 132–162.

946
Watch your purse
Financial stress can taint times that should be relaxing. Weeks before the run-up to a big day, plan what needs to be bought and see how much you have to spend. If the two don't tally, can you cut back to avoid absorbing the stress of a loan?

947
What is Christmas about?
Sit quietly, close your eyes and contemplate what these words mean: "…on earth peace, good will toward men" (St Luke 2.14). How can you bring more of this sentiment into your life and the lives of loved ones in the coming year? Write an angelic message to yourself.

Make a gift of deliciously more-ish olives.

948
Get religious
Try a religious service to get back to the source when you're feeling frazzled. What it's all about in the end, however non-religious your beliefs, is how a baby can bring peace and hope to the world. Encourage children to gain a perspective deeper than present-getting by taking them to a Christingle service (it involves sweets and candles).

949
Do something together
Throw a homemade tree party. Ask family or friends around for a "making" afternoon and spend it cutting, folding, gluing and glittering enough decorations to cover a tree, including a fairy or star for the top. When everything is dry, decorate the tree. You get to spend time laughing and reminiscing with those you love and a chore gets done.

Let go of stress during hectic festivities with some uplifting group singing.

950
Sing with others
Religious and secular celebrations gain a spark from singing in unison. Organize a group to sing from door to door, go to a carol service, or croon along to a guitar when stress gets you down. Singing blocks the neural pathways along which pain travels, boosts memory and energy levels and helps you to breathe effectively and stand better. When a group in Germany sang Mozart's *Requiem,* their levels of immunity-boosting immunoglobulin A soared.

951
Chill a while
The world is unlikely to end over Christmas, so don't feel you need to see everyone before 1 January.

952
Warring factions
Having a focus at family functions is a good way to hold down tension. Organize games with two teams, such as board games, carpet skittles or, even better, do something really physical outdoors, such as a game of cricket or softball. Whatever you do, don't use the time to try to solve long-standing rivalry – and don't serve too much booze!

953
Do something charitable
Invite a lonely neighbour to eat with you, offer your help at a homeless shelter, grin at that joke you've heard a million times since childhood and avoid topics that wind up your anarchist niece.

954
Don't feel guilty
If this is a bad time of year because of loss, separation or loneliness, don't feel guilty, advises the American Psychological Association (APA). And don't feel alone – the Christmas-card happy family is rare. The APA suggests being gentle with yourself, asking for informal, community or professional support, and considering volunteering, an effective way to make yourself feel more connected and needed.

955
Write a letter
Loss is hard at this time of year. If it helps, write your loved one a letter explaining your feelings, which might include guilt for abandoning old traditions or enjoying yourself.

956
Make up
Can you ask yourself why you're lonely now? Is there anything you could say to people from the past to change the situation? What could you do to widen your network?

957
Families apart
At celebration times, try to put righteous indignation and hurt to one side after separation – and try

not to take "snubs" to heart at this time of heightened emotion. Family psychologists suggest creating new rituals in which each person has a role to help you step out of the shadow of previous partners. This can bring new families closer together and helps everyone cope with the stress of wanting things to be as they were before.

958
Save the children

If your family is scattered, try to shift the weight of responsibility of where to go away from children, who may worry that they have to keep everybody happy if asked to choose where to spend a special time. Children may feel less like pawns if you simply take turns in where they go each year.

959
Family meeting

Whatever kind of family you are part of, think about holding a family meeting to decide what each of you would like to do at special times of the year and to discuss why all of you may need to make compromises. Ask yourselves why you keep doing the stuff that winds you up. Once you are clear about everyone's expectations, where you will all be and who you will be with, you can start to talk and build excitement about the big day.

960
Me time

If you're holding it all together on the surface, but are seething underneath, give yourself some time on your own to have a cry, chat to the significant other who isn't there or take the dog for a long walk.

961
Help me now

Don't forget Rescue Remedy. It has Bach Flower Essences to counter trauma, panic, irritability, "headless-chicken busyness", loss of contact

with reality and a general fear of losing it altogether. That just about covers all the possible outcomes of a relaxed family Christmas!

962
Time of transition

Mark the end of the year by raising a glass to the positive elements of the last year – the new people and places that came into your life and your growth at home, work and within. Think also about people and activities that dropped away. How does this make you feel and how can you change your life for the better?

Welcome in the New Year with a toast to new friends and circumstances.

Effortless partying

Parties keep us connected with the people we care about – it's this social connection that buffers us so effectively against stress. But they can be so unrelaxing to organize that you might stop holding them. Here are some destressing tips for before, during and after. Alternatively, you could call in party planners, caterers and cleaners...

Easy-to-prepare food leaves you time to sit back and enjoy the party.

963
Don't be a martyr
A party is too much work for one person, even if you have immaculate to-do lists. Call in friends to help, allocating tasks such as invitations, RSVPing, cleaning, shopping, organizing drinks, glasses, ice, plates, decorations, flowers, sounds, lighting, parking and cleaning again.

964
Keep things simple
People want to see your face, not your sweaty back as you run in and out of the kitchen fetching, carrying and preparing elaborate creations. Go for something in a pot that goes from oven to table – a casserole or curry served with bread or rice.

965
Don't cook
If cooking is stressful, ask guests to bring a dish (have one of them co-ordinate) or buy cheeses, cold meats and great bread and throw together salads and fruit. If you're worried about asking people to bring food, create a theme – sushi, curry, paella, fajitas – and call it a competition. This is guaranteed to get the men cooking. You just provide the prize.

966
Choose specialities
Serve something you couldn't make yourself, bought from a patisserie, smokery or other specialist artisan. You get the kudos for being a foodie and support local craftspeople.

967
Support local breweries
Ask if a local brewer or winemaker will supply your party (and send staff to serve gratis). This wipes out many time-consuming tasks such as shopping, selecting, carrying and serving, as well as cutting down on your food miles and supporting the local economy. How very relaxing on so many levels.

968
Sugar is best
An Australian study from 2006 found that artificial sweeteners in diet versions of mixers cause the alcohol in drinks to pass into the bloodstream even faster. People in the study who drank a shot of vodka with a regular mixer stayed within the limit for driving; those who drank the same amount of vodka with a diet mixer veered over the limit. To prevent regrets the following morning, stick to non-diet sugary mixers.

969
Prepare your feet
To save your feet from stress if you're not used to wearing high heels, try this yoga tip, which resembles what little girls do when they play princesses. Come up onto your tiptoes – try to come almost vertical so your ankles are directly over your toes. Hold the position if

you can. Now walk around the room slowly, with each step rising as high onto your tiptoes as possible. If you can practise with a book balanced on your head, even better.

970
Look good

Make sure you set aside enough time to prepare a show-stopping outfit. If it's your party, you should look the best there. Take a friend shopping if you're unsure. Or if this makes you feel uneasy, go for fabulous new underwear and shoes.

971
Combat puffy eyes

Make a pot of camomile tea using two tea bags, then sip the tea. When cool, wring out the bags and recline with one bag on each eye. This is calming for tired skin and eyes and a nervous tummy before a big event.

972
Plan a pamper session

Don't be there to feel hassled before the party starts. Instead, find a beauty salon that offers party-pamper appointments. Treat yourself to a facial, pedicure and manicure and get your hair done as you sip champagne and wind up gently into party mood.

973
Arrive late

Get the venue ready, then have someone else be there to greet arriving guests while you go off for that pamper session. Arrive one hour in so that you lose an hour of worrying about whether anyone will actually turn up.

974
Homemade lemonade

This recipe is straightforward, but looks impressive and tastes delicious. The refreshing, zesty lemon taste makes it a perfect beverage for lazy summer afternoon gatherings.

- 1 large unwaxed lemon
- 25g caster sugar
- ice
- handful fresh mint leaves

1 Zest the lemon using a lemon zester, being careful not to peel away the bitter white pith. Place the zested rind in a large glass jug.

2 Squeeze the lemon and pour the juice into the jug. Add the sugar, then pour over enough boiling water to dissolve the sugar, stirring well.

3 Top up the jug with cold water and place in the fridge to cool before serving. Once cooled, add the ice and the mint sprigs.

Blowing bubbles never fails to delight.

975
Headache pressure point

If your head starts to pulsate, try pressing the back of your hand with your opposite thumb, placing it between the base of your thumb and first finger in the natural groove between the bones. You may find a painful spot. Hold it and feel the pain clearing.

976
Herbal headache remedy

Chewing feverfew leaves (*Tanacetum parthenium*) can prevent headaches and even migraines. Or take 5–10 drops of the tincture in water every 30 minutes or so at the onset of a headache. (Avoid with blood-thinning medication or in pregnancy.)

977
Homeopathy for tension headaches

Have some homeopathic remedies to hand to combat party-stress headaches.
• Cocculus 30 for the classic headache stemming from lack of sleep that starts in the nape of the neck and moves into the back of the head, accompanied by confusion and nausea. (Take a dose and go back to bed!)
• Kali.Phos 30 for headaches at the back of the head caused by stress or overwork; this remedy suits the chronically stressed out.
• China 30 for a horrible headache brought on by nervous strain, which mainly comprises waves of throbbing through the whole head.

978
Children's party pressure

The pressure is on parents to throw huge parties inviting the whole class, which means hiring a hall, entertainer, face painter and bouncy castle – ratcheting up the pressure for the next parent. Just say no! Ditch the themes. Avoid plastic parties and stop passing on social competitiveness to another generation. Instead, invite six friends around for a birthday tea and play games. Try the old favourites, such as pass the parcel, musical statues, and pin the tail on the donkey.

979
Party bag madness

Kids expect party bags. It makes them avaricious. Say no. Instead, get them to make something they can take home: perhaps threading beads to make jewellery (buy letter beads so they can spell words), decorating a hat or threading beads and buttons onto a wire to bend into heart and fish shapes and hang as a mobile.

980
Ten calming kids' games

• Send them into the garden with pots of bubbles.
• Who can keep a feather in the air longest by blowing?
• Let older children plan a game.
• Have them dance to slow classical

music (prince/princess music).

- Who can lie still the longest?
- Put down a huge piece of paper on the floor and let everyone contribute to a picture.

• Play a whispering game.

• Take the pace up and down.

• Blindfold sense game: fill bags with items that smell, taste or have a texture for kids to guess.

• Let them play on their own!

981

Making fairy dust

Essential for kids' parties – try running a trail around your garden for a treasure hunt. Also good on Christmas Eve for marking out a landing strip.

• Glitter dust – mix together 3 tbsp silver glitter and 2 tbsp rose-scented talcum powder in a bowl. Best scattered outside.

• Reindeer dust – mix together 3 tbsp foiled Christmas confetti with 2 tbsp pine needles.

• Midsummer magic – combine 1 tbsp each of rose petals and lavender florets. Mix in 1 tbsp pink glitter.

982

Whole body wind-down

This sequence brings you down if you can't come back to earth after a particularly lively night.

Lie down on your back next to a wall, then swivel round and, keeping your bottom close to the wall, raise the legs so that they are resting up against the wall (see No. 106).

Kneel about 30cm (1ft) in front of a sofa with your knees hip-width apart; try to place your bottom on the floor between your feet (if this feels difficult, pile cushions beneath your bottom until you are comfortable). Lie back on the sofa with your back and head completely supported (add pillows as necessary). Rest for 5 minutes, breathing gently. (Avoid if you have varicose veins or phlebitis.)

Now sit with the back of your pelvis, shoulders and head against a wall. Bring the soles of your feet together and let your knees flop out to the side. Draw your feet towards

you (see No. 670). Finally, lie on your back in a darkened room with an eye mask (see No. 321).

983

Herbs for hangovers

Although evening primrose oil is mainly known as a treatment for pre-menstrual tension, it is also an effective hangover cure. Take 2 capsules every 3–4 hours.

984

Feel better quick

Those who are sceptical about the efficacy of homeopathy should try Nux.Vom 30 hourly for a few hours when they have a hangover. This remedy has cured many people of scepticism as well as hangovers!

Don't be afraid to build in some "free-play" time at kids' parties.

Relaxing life lessons

Small changes make a big difference when it comes to leading a more relaxed life. If you consider these tips every day, you will feel less stressed and are likely to stay healthy and happy into old age – relaxing increases your lifespan.

985
Look at your core values

What do you want from life? Not a flat-screen TV or a new car – think about your values. Does your life reflect them? How could you make changes to reflect what's important?

986
Move your head

We spend our lives looking down – metaphorically as well as literally. Look forwards and at times upwards to relax posture, relieve tension in the shoulders and back and engage with nature and other people.

987
Things don't make us happy

We own more than our parents, but are not happier or more relaxed: a culture that equates possessions with social status and happiness is linked with rising anxiety, anger and frustration. Before you buy, ask if you need it. Value permanency, too – lust for items that have longevity and that you'll want to repair.

988
Create chaos

Take risks, throw caution to the wind and stir it up a bit at times to remind you that you are a sentient being. Jump off some metaphorical cliffs!

989
Do different

Try new ways to do business, enjoy your family and keep life stimulating, but make sure you stick to your principles and don't hurt people.

990
Learn new things

Each year learn a skill, every month listen to something new or go to an exhibition, each week greet a new person, every day use a new word.

991
Honour special moments

Build small moments of happiness into tasks that rile you. Researchers from University College London found that people who felt happy 33 times in a day had 32 per cent lower levels of the stress hormone cortisol than those who didn't feel happy.

992
Get outside yourself

Whether through sport, poetry, walking, playing with children or cooking, live in the here and now and find a place where you are you. This is anger management, meditation, respite and recuperation.

993
Celebrate relationships

Psychologists suggest doing one thing a day to make a union stronger: some say this is more crucial to health than exercise. It might be getting married: married people relax more than those in long-term partnerships.

994
Think about God

The orthodox church urges us to drop the mind into the heart and stand before God. Be aware of that divine presence, whatever you call it.

995
Just breathe

At moments of stress, close your eyes, put your hands on the abdomen and follow your breath as it moves your hands up and down. Do nothing else with your body or your mind.

996
Eat Mediterranean

Base your diet around plenty of fresh fruit and vegetables, whole grains, fish, olive oil and yogurt, with smaller amounts of meat and red wine. Most relaxing of all, cook dishes yourself from scratch, and eat sitting at a table, putting down your knife and fork between bites.

997
Exercise

Just half an hour of daily activity that leaves you slightly breathless protects the body, mind and emotions from the negative consequences of stress. Walking, cycling, housework and gardening seem to be more effective than a burst of high-impact exercise at the gym, suggests a study from Maastricht University.

998
Be receptive

Open yourself up to what life has to offer with the meditation *mudra* (hand gesture). Sit or kneel with your eyes closed and rest your hands gently in your lap with your palms upright, one cupped softly inside the other, fingers aligned and thumbs almost touching (imagine a grain of rice between them) to make an oval near your navel (see right). Sense how this makes you feel open and yet completely at peace.

999
Just smile

Feeling optimistic can reduce your blood pressure and heart rate and reduces your risk of heart disease, according to a University of Pittsburgh study. It also boosts immunity and lifespan, and makes you look less stressed – as the reggae singer U-Roy toasts, "Smile a while and give your face a rest."

1000
Turn off your brain

When your brain is frazzled, let your body take over by doing something that can't be learned intellectually, but has to be intuited. Hula-hooping is great, or jumping a rope while two people turn it. Or try chopping wood for a fire for the evening. Measuring yourself against something real brings real serenity.

1001
Where is home?

Stop fleeing your home at weekends and evenings. Decide where's home and live there.

To shrink your world to manageable proportions, get to know who sleeps on the other side of the walls, and who runs shops, cafés and schools. Travel by foot and get information by talking to people and visiting libraries. Communities are more caring if you live with neighbours rather than a distant clique.

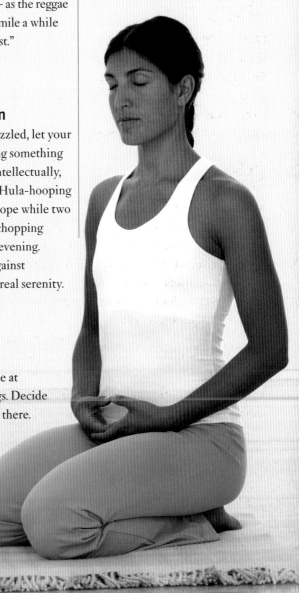

Resources

Yoga
• www.allaboutyoga.co.uk
• yoga equipment: www.yogamatters.com
• Iyengar association of Great Britain: www.iyengaryoga.org.uk
• UK yoga directory: www.yoga.co.uk
• British Wheel of Yoga: www.bwy.org.uk

T'ai chi
• www.taichiunion.com

Pilates
• www.pilatesfoundation.com

Homeopathy
• Society of Homeopaths: www.homeopathy-soh.org
• British Institute of Homeopathy: www.britinsthom.com

Green organisations
• www.thegreenorganisation.info
• www.seventhgeneration.com
• www.ecoverproducts.co.uk
• www.organicfood.co.uk
• www.soilassociation.org
• www.ramblers.org.uk

Meditation
• www.therapy-world.co.uk/medit.htm
• Transcendental meditation - www.t-m.org.uk

Retreats
• www.theretreatcompany.co.uk
• www.IntegralLifeCentre.org
• www.yogaholidays.net

Surfing
• www.britsurf.co.uk

Breastfeeding
• La Leche league: www.laleche.org.uk

Index

About the author

Susannah Marriott is a freelance writer who specializes in complementary healthcare. She is the author of 15 illustrated books on yoga, spa treatments, meditation and prayer, and natural approaches to pregnancy and parenting, including *Total Meditation, Basic Yoga, The Art of the Bath, Your Non-Toxic Pregnancy* and *1001 Ways to Stay Young Naturally*. Her writing has appeared in *Weekend Guardian* and *The Times, Zest, Top Sante, Healthy, She* and *Junior* and she has broadcast on BBC Radio 4. Susannah lives with her husband and three young daughters in Cornwall, where she lectures on writing at University College Falmouth. She relaxes by practising yoga, swimming in the Atlantic, holidaying in a camper van and dancing to very loud jazz.

Acknowledgments

Author's acknowledgments

Special thanks to Amanda Brown and Julia Lightfoot. Thanks to Mat and Sue Johnstone-Clarke for tips on horticultural and foraging; Kate Holiday for the fire-lighting and olive recipe; Rosie Hadden for dating, communities, grieving and moonwalking; Kelly Thompson for destressing at work; alisailments.blogspot. com and the Round Chapel in Hackney for spiritual inspiration; Richard Trayford for horses; Ian and Hazel Potter for cricket; Emily Apple for direct action; Judy Hemingsley for homeworking; Andy Cox for surfing and lifesaving; Jen Wight for climbing; David and Dominic Bate for Burns' Night.
Thanks to Carole and Claire, Penny and Peggy at DK. And to everyone at home, especially my husband, for time to write and a house filled with music.

Contributors

Julia Linfoot BSc MCPH MARH is a Registered Homeopath in practice in South London since 1999. She also prescribes herbal tinctures, flower essences and tissue salts. She supervises student homeopaths, and teaches courses in homeopathy and health.

Bellenden Therapies: tel: 0207 732 1417; email: juliahomeopath@btinternet.com

Amanda Brown has been teaching yoga for 17 years. She also practises as an artist and a natural therapist.
Tel: 01326 318776
email: magicbean_99@yahoo.co.uk

Publisher's acknowledgments

Dorling Kindersley would like to thank Alyson Silverwood for proof-reading and Michèle Clarke for the index.
They would also like to thank Ruth Jenkinson for the new photography, Alli Williams for hair and make-up and Liz Hippisley for styling.
Thanks also to Aromatherapy oils: Neal's Yard Remedies, mail order 0845 262 3145
Yoga mats: Yoga Matters, www. yogamatters.com +44 (0)20 8888 0623
Yoga clothes: Asquith London, www. asquithlondon.com +44(0) 20 8968 3100
Exercise clothes: Sweaty Betty, www.sweatyBetty.com
Models: Kate Loustau and Nicola Wallace from Close Agency; Kevin Harris from Model Plan Agency; Nina Malone, Tara Lee, Stevie Hope and Susannah Marriott.